W9-ACD-305

Painting Zoo Animals on Rocks

Lin Wellford

NORTH LIGHT BOOKS
CINCINNATI, OHIO
www.artistsnetwork.com

About the Author

After a childhood in Florida, living in the Arkansas Ozarks gave Lin Wellford a true appreciation for all the wonderful rocks and stones that line creek beds, beaches and country roads there and all over the world. She's developed a missionary's zeal for spreading the word that rock painting is not only an inexpensive and exciting art form, but also a fabulous tool for helping people discover and connect with their own creative natures.

The popularity of her "rock books" has been a pleasant surprise, leading to television appearances and other opportunities to spread the word about rocks as a fabulous art material for people of all ages and abilities.

The mother of three grown daughters, Lin continues to paint, write and collect rocks in Green Forest, Arkansas.

Painting Zoo Animals on Rocks. Copyright © 2004 by Lin Wellford. Manufactured in China. All rights reserved. The patterns and drawings in the book are for personal use of the reader. By permission of the author and publisher, they may be either hand-traced or photocopied to make single copies, but under no circumstances may they be resold or republished. It is permissible for the purchaser to make the projects contained herein and sell them at fairs, bazaars and craft shows. No other part of this book may be reproduced in any form or by any electronic or mechanical means including information storage and retrieval systems without permission in writing from the publisher, except by a reviewer, who may quote a brief passage in review. Published by North Light Books, an imprint of F&W Publications, Inc., 4700 East Galbraith Road, Cincinnati, Ohio 45236. (800) 289-0963. First edition.

08 07 06 05 04   5 4 3 2 1

Library of Congress Cataloging-in-Publication Data
Wellford, Lin
   Painting zoo animals on rocks / Lin Wellford.
      p. cm
   ISBN 1-58180-465-2 (alk. paper)
      1. Stone painting. 2. Acrylic painting. 3. Animals in art I. Title.
   TT370.W6528 2004
   751.4'26–dc22
                                          2003066212

Editor: Christine Doyle
Cover Designer: Marissa Bowers
Interior Designer: Camille De Rhodes
Production Coordinator: Sara Dumford
Cover Photographer: Al Parrish
Interior Photography by Lin Wellford

metric conversion chart

To Convert	To	Multiply By
Inches	Centimeters	2.54
Centimeters	Inches	0.4
Feet	Centimeters	30.5
Centimeters	Feet	0.03
Yards	Meters	0.9
Meters	Yards	1.1
Sq. Inches	Sq. Centimeters	6.45
Sq. Centimeters	Sq. Inches	0.16
Sq. Feet	Sq. Meters	0.09
Sq. Meters	Sq. Feet	10.8
Sq. Yards	Sq. Meters	0.8
Sq. Meters	Sq. Yards	1.2
Pounds	Kilograms	0.45
Kilograms	Pounds	2.2
Ounces	Grams	28.3
Grams	Ounces	0.035

Dedication

To my family and to devoted animal lovers everywhere who are working to preserve our planet's precious diversity.

Table of Contents

14 | Welcome to the Zoo

100 | Welcome to the Petting Zoo

Introduction

Animals had always intrigued me. Then I married a man who shares my fascination with wildlife. As our kids were growing up, we planned family vacations around adding new zoos to our list, from large and well-known institutions, like the National Zoo in Washington, D.C. and the St. Louis Zoo, to smaller, more intimate regional and local collections like the Dickerson Park Zoo in nearby Springfield, Missouri. What we discovered is that each zoo has its own distinct personality and unique mix of animals. Because the inhabitants are unpredictable, even the same zoo offers a different experience with each visit. My family vividly recalls the time a male ostrich took a shine to one of our daughters and did a wildly animated mating dance just for her. At a zoo in Germany, we watched in amazement as a woman bustled into the glass-windowed primate enclosure where orangutans and gorillas were lying about in total lethargy. At the sight of her, the apes perked up and began to gather at the windows. She proceeded to take items out of a bulging canvas bag and hold them up for her rapt audience.

"These are intelligent animals," she explained to my husband as she slowly displayed each item, turning it over and around. "All day long people come to look at the animals. I bring new things for them to look at, and they are always so excited."

Encounters like these reveal that zoos offer the opportunity not just to look but also to interact with a variety of animals from all over the world in ways that would not otherwise be possible.

This book is a celebration of the diversity and wonder of the animal world. Without zoos and their dedicated keepers and supporters, our exposure to so many animals would be limited to photographs in books and programs on television.

Getting Started

Even if you have never painted before, painting on rocks offers the opportunity to achieve surprisingly realistic results. We live in a dimensional world, so fitting an animal onto an object with a distinct shape is like taking a shortcut to painting success. Unlike traditional flat surfaces, rocks have no background or foreground, and no blank expanse to stymie the beginner. Instead, a rock's compact shape more or less dictates what can go where.

As you develop a feel for how the shape of a rock enhances the illusion of realism, you will find that this art form offers a very natural way to build skills and abilities you may not realize you possess.

Often, fear of failure is the biggest stumbling block people face when it comes to creative activities. It is a relief to realize that not only is it impossible to "ruin" a rock, but that this is a very forgiving medium. If you do something you don't like, simply dampen the paint before it dries and lift away the mistake with a paper towel. Or wait until the problem area is dry and paint over it. There is no such thing as a mistake you can't fix.

Finding Rocks

Before you can begin, though, you need a supply of rocks. It may be helpful to look at the rock shapes used for various projects in this book first. Study the way preliminary sketches were fitted onto certain rocks so that when you begin looking for your own rocks, you will have a clearer idea of shapes and sizes.

The easiest rocks to paint are those that are basically smooth, with edges and angles that have been tumbled and rounded, usually as the result of ocean tides or river currents. I find most of my rocks on the banks of a local creek. On occasion I have bought good painting rocks at rock yards that supply building and landscaping materials. If you live in an area where water-tumbled rocks are not naturally available, buying them is an acceptable option, and you will find the cost is minimal, especially when compared to most art materials.

For some of the projects in this book, I used small pebbles or gravel pieces from my driveway to enhance the rock's shape. Pebbles and gravel are even easier to find than larger rocks.

My rock pile does double duty as a landscaping element!

Drawing or Tracing the Designs

If you are not confident about your drawing abilities, that need not keep you from enjoying rock painting. Many of the project animals can be broken down into elementary geometric shapes. Another option is to trace or scan the design and use a computer or copy machine to enlarge or reduce the image to fit the rock chosen for it. Cut out the design and glue it onto cardstock, then trim slightly inside the lines, creating a reusable template. By cutting out the eye circles and perhaps even the nose, you ensure perfect placement. To use the template, press the template firmly on the rock and trace around the shape.

Ordinary graphite pencils can be used for drawing on many projects. Others require a white-leaded or white charcoal pencil, which can be found at art supply stores, or a soapstone pen, available where sewing supplies are sold. This pen is also used by welders and sold in large hardware and home centers.

In keeping with the uncomplicated nature of this art form, a very small number of brushes are all that's needed to achieve great results.

Supplies

Brushes

A wide variety of brushes can be used on rocks. Many of my rocks are sandstone and have a surface that is similar to fine sandpaper, so I prefer to use inexpensive stiff, white bristled brushes that I can sometimes find in sets at "dollar" stores or other bargain stores. These are perfect for applying basecoats and scrubbing on paint with a dry brush. Scruffy and worn brushes can be excellent for scrubbing on paint, so don't throw them away until they are worn down to nubs! For fine details and fur lines, my favorite brush is Loew-Cornell's liner in the 7050 series. The no. 0 or no. 1 is long enough to carry a lot of paint but fine enough to make very delicate lines. Loew-Cornell's 7300-C shader in sizes 4 and 6 are also used for some of the projects in this book as is the ⅜ inch (10mm) 7400-C angular shader.

When painting fur, you may want to use a rake or comb brush designed to make multiple fur lines in a single stroke. You can even create your own customized version by snipping sections from an inexpensive flat brush like I did to the brush on the left.

Paints

Any brand of acrylic paint can be used. If you plan to display your rocks outside, DecoArt's Patio Paint brand of acrylic paint is specifically formulated to resist fading and weathering. Because it is designed to use on porous surfaces, it may not adhere as well to extremely hard or smooth rocks. I found that a coat of Kilz, a primer used to prepare surfaces for subsequent painting, creates an excellent basecoat that prevents peeling or flaking that occurs on some rock types.

Other Supplies

Here are a few more basic supplies you'll need for successful rock painting. And other supplies, while not necessary, may make your painting easier and more fun.

To sketch or trace the designs onto your rocks you'll need a regular pencil for light-colored rocks and a white-leaded or white charcoal pencil or soapstone pen for darker rocks. Soapstone pens are available through suppliers of welding materials or at home improvement stores.

To make templates for the patterns in this book, you'll need scissors, tracing paper, cardstock and glue.

A turntable or lazy Susan on which to place your rock makes painting in the round much simpler.

Wood fillers may be used to correct an uneven base or fill in a hole or crack in your rock. You can also use it to make extensions to your rocks like I do to make giraffes (see page 91). The wood filler I use most is Leech Real Wood Filler.

Cement bond is also used to make the giraffe's neck extension. I use Bond 527 Multi-Purpose Cement in these projects. Combined with the wood filler, the cement bond makes the extension extremely durable. One reason the bond is so secure is that there seems to be a chemical reaction between the two products. Something in the wood filler causes the glue to soften slightly then reset even harder than before.

A clear acrylic spray sealer will enrich your colors and protect the surface of your rocks after you're done painting them.

Patio Paint is formulated for outdoor use and comes in dozens of colors, but my palette is usually limited to a handful of basic colors.

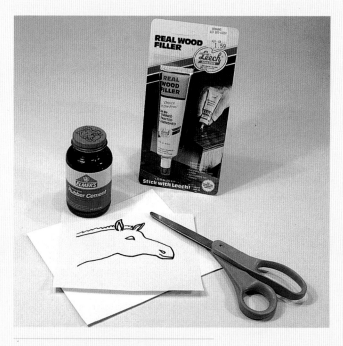

In addition to paints and brushes, a few other supplies will be handy. Wood filler is used to make an even base on your rock. The other supplies above, scissors, tracing paper, cardstock and glue, can be used to make templates. Glue the traced designs to the cardstock, making a sturdy template for repeated use.

Techniques

For most rock painting projects, there are a few simple painting techniques that will help you achieve attractive and realistic results.

Holding the Brush

New painters sometimes aren't sure how best to control the brush to paint fine details and fur. The best way to do this is to hold your brush upright, almost perpendicular to the surface of the rock. Try using your pinkie finger to anchor your hand to the rock as you paint for additional stability and control.

Getting Proper Paint Consistency

Beginners often struggle to get the consistency of their paint right. Usually you will need to add increments of water to your paint to achieve a consistency that allows you to make clear, crisp lines. Water allows the paint to flow smoothly off the tip of the brush bristles. Too much water, however, will make the strokes fade as they dry. Paint that is too thick will clot on the brush, causing broken lines or fuzzy strokes rather than the cleanly defined lines you need. Once the paint is right, you should be able to make at least three or four sets of lines between refills, perhaps many more.

Practicing on newsprint can be a great help. I always lay newspaper on my work surface. It protects my tabletop and also provides the perfect testing surface for checking the consistency of paint for brushstrokes.

Drybrushing

Shadows and highlights are two elements that lend to the realism of the zoo animals in this book. And they're easy to paint with drybrushing. Use a stiff or worn-to-the-nub brush and fairly dry paint to drybrush, or scrub, the pigment into place. Drybrushing yields a soft, diffused look without sharp edges or noticeable brushstrokes.

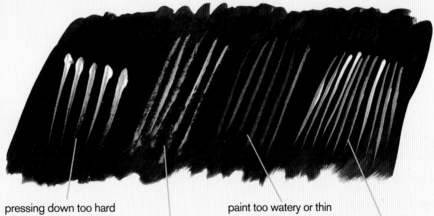

pressing down too hard at beginning of stroke

paint too thick or too dry

paint too watery or thin

crisp, distinct lines

Here I've highlighted the rock using drybrushing. This technique leaves the edges softly diffused.

Painting Fur

Your zoo animals will really come to life when they are painted with lifelike fur. Use a liner brush to paint one hair at a time, or use a rake or comb brush to paint multiple lines at once. Thin the paint as described on page 11 and use the following techniques and suggestions.

Outline With Splinter Strokes: Very short, very thin strokes painted in dense rows are what I refer to as splinter strokes. Use them to define important features while adding furry texture to the piece.

Layer Fur Lines: For large areas of fur, create a row of longer strokes, then move halfway up and make another row that overlaps the first. Successive overlapping layers will create the unbroken look of a realistic coat for your animal.

Cluster Fur Strokes: For a different fur effect, cluster sets of strokes that fan out slightly. Each set remains distinct from those around it. This produces wavy fur.

Follow Fur Growth Guide: Every animal's fur grows in a distinctive way. By following the patterns provided in the projects that show fur growth direction, you will be able to paint fur that is natural and lifelike. Refer to these patterns frequently as you paint the fur.

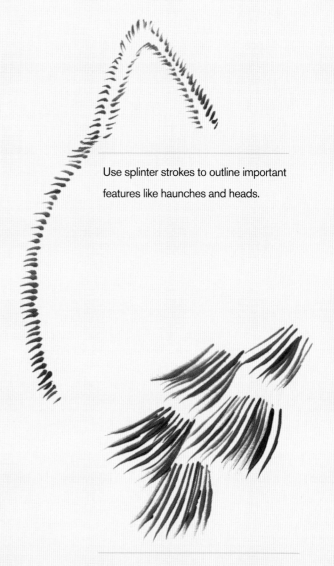

Use splinter strokes to outline important features like haunches and heads.

Clustering strokes and giving them curved ends will produce wavy fur.

By layering your fur lines, your animal's fur will look full and lifelike.

A fur direction guide, like this one, will accompany the furrier zoo animals in this book. Refer to them as you paint the fur or consult close-up pictures of the actual animal.

Tinting Fur

Tinting is a helpful technique for softening or altering fur colors. Like hair dye, a tint is a transparent color brushed over part of the animal. The light areas that are washed over will be tinted by the color; the dark areas will be unaffected. To make a tint, thin the paint with water until it is loose and transparent.

Augmenting Rocks

While rocks already have dimension, augmenting the rock's shape is a dramatic way of achieving even more realism. Previously, the only way to alter rock was with a chisel and mallet, physically removing rock to get the desired effect. But I discovered an easy and exciting way to change the shapes of my rocks using bits of gravel, glue and wood filler. These additions are surprisingly sturdy and open up a whole new world of creativity. For step-by-step instructions for augmenting rocks, see the giraffe project, page 88.

A thin wash of paint adds a subtle tint to these fur lines.

With some pieces of gravel, glue and wood filler, you can augment a rock to create even more dimension. Here I'm creating a neck for a giraffe.

Getting Inspired

Good photo resources will enhance the quality of your rock painting, so begin collecting pictures of animals that can help you get the most realistic look in your work.

As with all creative activities, practice will help you perfect your techniques. But transforming ordinary rocks into works of art is such a fun and exciting activity that it feels almost magical. You may be amazed at how quickly rock painting transforms you into an artist!

Welcome to the Zoo

Zoos have changed a great deal over the past century as more was learned about animals in the wild. Once our primitive zoos were little more than prison cells where the inmates spent their days restlessly pacing as visitors peered at them through narrow bars. Now much effort is put into creating display areas that are spacious and natural looking. Bars have been replaced by less obvious barriers, and naturalists study wildlife behavior and look for ways to stimulate and enrich the environment for every animal under their care. These changes allow zoo visitors to get a much clearer idea of how different animals live and interact with one another in the wild. Many zoos also serve as breeding facilities devoted to maintaining dwindling populations of endangered species. No longer prisons, our well-run, modern zoos are sanctuaries and havens aiming to ensure that each precious inhabitant is allowed to enjoy a decent quality of life even as they add so much enjoyment to ours.

Big Cat Country

It's hard to imagine a zoo without a lion exhibit. Even when they are relaxed, these

animals retain a majestic air that seems to define the term "animal magnetism."

The male's flowing mane gives this big cat his distinction, and it can be painted

either tawny, dark brown or even black. Though lacking the male's handsome

mane, the lioness shares his strong and striking features and bearing. Paint several

lions and group them together for maximum effect.

what you'll need

DecoArt Patio Paint in Patio Brick • Wrought Iron Black •
Sunflower Yellow • Cloud White • medium stiff-bristled brushes
• small and medium flat brushes • no. 0 or no. 1 liner brush •
rake or grass comb, optional • soapstone pen or white-leaded
pencil • template-making supplies, as listed on page 10, optional
• clear acrylic spray sealer

1| Choosing a Rock

To find a suitable rock for this majestic animal, look for one that has a wedge shape, with a flat bottom and a top that angles upward before leveling off to form a broadly rounded top. Make sure there is ample space for the head. All of these rocks would be great lions, and I chose the center rock for this project.

2| Preparing the Surface

Scrub your rock and let it dry, then basecoat the entire visible surface with Patio Brick. A stiff-bristled, flat brush allows quick coverage of the basecoat.

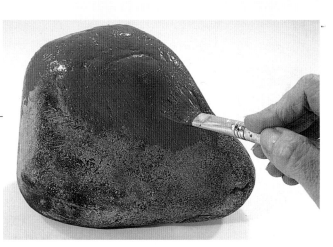

3| Sketch the Design

After the basecoat dries, sketch on the guidelines or use a template as described on page 9, using a soapstone pen or white-leaded pencil. Because the features are made up of mostly geometric shapes, this animal is easy to draw following the steps below and on the opposite page.

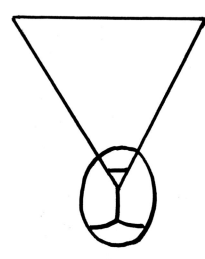
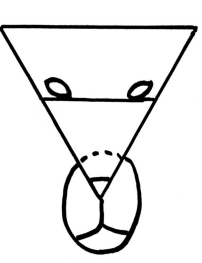
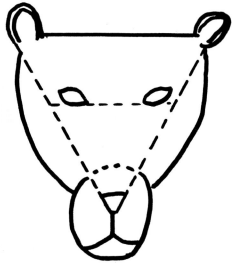

Sketch an inverted triangle just below the top of the rock. The bottom tip of this triangle forms the lion's nose leather. Encircle the nose with an oval that becomes the muzzle and chin. Draw a straight line down and angle two lines out for the mouth.

Evenly bisect the large triangle head shape with a horizontal line. Set two widely spaced almond-shaped eyes on the line that bisects the large triangle.

At the top corners of the head triangle, add two rounded ears. Curve a cheek line down from the lower edge of each ear to join the muzzle oval not quite halfway down.

Gently curve the legs as shown, rather than making them straight across, and give the paws a rounded shape. Here, I'm drawing the design with soapstone; the guidelines show up well but are easy to erase if corrections are needed.

If painting a male lion, draw lines radiating from the head for the mane. Move down to the small end of the rock and sketch in a haunch and a rear foot. Curve the tail around from the end of the rock so that it overlaps the bottom of the haunch. The tip ends above the toes of the rear foot. Add an elongated foreleg that starts just past the tail and ends below the head.

These drawings are patterns as well as fur direction guides. Refer to them as you paint the fur so that your lion's fur will look natural.

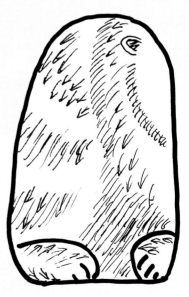

On the backside of the rock make a matching haunch shape with a straight rear leg showing, and a front leg with the paw tucked in to create an elongated oval.

4| Establish Contours

Mix just enough black paint into Patio Brick to make a deep chocolate brown. Use a stiff-bristled, medium-sized brush to create the outlines and shadows that will establish the lion's dimension. Begin by filling in the centers of the rounded ear shapes. Surround the lower portion of the head by stroking outward along the guidelines from ear to ear. These short strokes should give the shadows feathered edges. Outline around the haunch on both the front and backside with smooth lines. Make thinner but still bold outlines around the tail and paws.

Move to the outside edges of the mane and darken in the area below the head and around the front paws. Follow the mane, stroking outward to create a feathery look. As you near the ears, narrow the width of the shadows. Work around the ears to the top of the head, curving in to touch the forehead. Then continue around the other side of the head. Finally, paint a triangle above the inverted triangle you drew on the lion's nose.

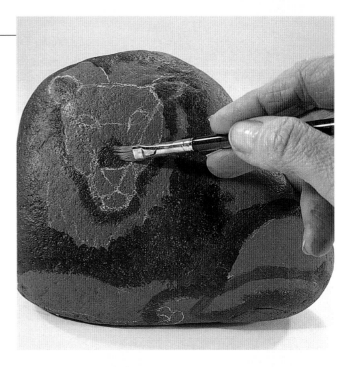

5| Add Soft Highlights

Mix equal parts Sunflower Yellow and white to get a pale golden color. Use a small to medium flat brush to create a partial mask around the eyes. Fill in the crescents between the curving cheek lines and the original triangle shape of the head, feathering the edges slightly where they overlap the face shadows. Also fill in the muzzle on either side of the nose leather, but give these areas smooth edges.

Pick up more paint, then wipe the brush to remove most of the paint from the brush. Drybrush highlights along the tops of the feet, along the top half of both haunches and the top half of the tail. Highlight the top of the lion's back, starting just beyond the shadows behind the head so that a narrow margin of plain basecoat remains. Paint the highlights heaviest along the tops of these areas and gradually diminish as you move downward, producing a diffused look without harsh edges.

6| Paint Dark Details

Switch to a liner brush and mix black with a small amount of Patio Brick to get a very deep brown that's nearly black. Use it to paint in curving toe lines and V-shaped claw tips on the front paws. If there is enough of the rear paw showing, give it three toe pads and a central pad. Next use the tip of your brush to go around the eye shapes. Outline the triangular nose and the lines that define the mouth. Also go around the outside edges of the muzzle to make them stand out.

7| Paint Light Details

Rinse your liner brush then mix one small drop of Sunflower Yellow with three drops of white to get a pale gold clearly lighter than the color used on the highlights. Begin along the tops of the front legs, painting very dense, short fur lines that slant toward the paw along the top edge. Paint another fringe of short fur lines along the lower edge of the paw's dry-brushed highlighting so that the tips of the fur extend slightly beyond it. Check the fur direction chart on page 19 for guidance. Add slanting fur lines to the top of the tail, as well as to the tip. On the front haunch begin at the top of the curve and add strokes to the side of the haunch but stop before reaching the tail. Go back to the top of the haunch and begin to work down, creating layers of fur until the last row extends slightly beyond the dry-brushed highlighting.

8| Use the Rake for the Fur

To more quickly paint the layers of fur, use the rake brush or your customized flat brush (see page 9). They require paint thinned slightly with water. Using these brushes takes some practice, but they can speed up the process considerably. You can also use your liner brush as before.

9| Add Fur to the Back

Paint fur lines along the back to provide texture and to blend the edges of dry-brushed highlights and the edges of shadow, rendering the differences between light and dark areas more subtle.

10 | Paint Fur Details on the Face

Use a liner and the lighter pale gold fur color to add short lines to the face. Start with a fringe along the edges of the mask surrounding the eyes. Then outline the rims of the ears with solid lines, and stroke in fur above the top of the forehead to indicate the upper reaches of the mane. Concentrate your lines along the bottom and the top, leaving the center of the forehead plain for now. Bring some fur down the center of the mask to soften the edges of the dark patch above the nose. Extend lines down either side of the nose to join the muzzle, leaving a narrow edge of brown basecoat in place so the muzzle is separate from the rest of the face. Move to the patches along either side of the face and use tiny splinter strokes to give the outside edges texture and to soften the contrast along the inside edges.

11 | Detail the Mane and Ruff

Still using the light paint, begin along the outer edges of the lower mane, stroking away from the face with a dense series of defining lines. Move inward with subsequent layers of overlapping strokes, making them sparser as you near the shadowed outlines of the face. Add extra fur lines to the bottom of the mane just above the two paws to suggest a ruff at the chest.

12 | Paint the Eyes

Use straight Sunflower Yellow to fill in the eyes, leaving the dark outlines surrounding them in place. Add a touch of Patio Brick to the yellow and give the top half of each eye a half circle of this deeper color. When dry, add black pupils that hang from the top center of the eyes in neatly shaped ovals.

13| Soften the Shadows With Dark Fur Lines

In the same way that lighter fur lines add texture to highlighted areas, dark brown (almost black) lines give shadowed areas texture. Using the liner brush, paint these lines with a mixture of black and a small amount of Patio Brick to get a deep brown shade. Concentrate these dark fur lines all the way around the outside edges of the mane.

14| Detail the Midsection

The area between the lion's mane and the curve of his haunch needs fur texture, too, but it should be lighter than the deep brown just used to set off the mane. Instead, mix equal parts Patio Brick and Sunflower Yellow to get a warm red-gold and use this to add several layers of sparse fur from the outside edges of the mane's shadows to the outside edges of the haunch shadows.

15| Make Adjustments

With the lower mane looking so lush, the upper mane seems out of balance, so I added more layers of pale gold fur to even the two areas out. Learning to use an "artist's eye" will help you see and correct similar imbalances.

16| Add Dark Fur Details to the Face

Mix Patio Brick and black to get a deep brown not quite as dark as that used to detail the shadows. Begin just below the area of plain basecoat in the center of the forehead, stroking up and away from the nose and fanning your strokes out as you move up to fill the area. Then use the tip of your brush to add small sets of short lines just above the eye on either side. These tiny lines add expression to your lion's face.

From there, move to the outside corner of each eye and extend a dark line out to the edge of the face on either side. Next add fur lines to the areas of plain basecoat below the eyes, letting the tips of your strokes extend like a fringe into the light areas along the sides of the face.

17| Add Dark Details Around the Head

Use the same brown color to detail the wedges of plain basecoat still showing where the mane joins the head. Stroke out and away from the shadow lines, using the dark lines to blend the dark areas into the lighter mane.

18| Detail Remaining Areas of Basecoat

Once the head and mane are done, look for other areas where the basecoat remains unfinished. These areas include the lower half of the legs and tail and the lower half of both the haunches. Consult the fur direction guide to ensure your fur is going in the direction it would naturally grow.

19| Add Fur Details on the Back and Sides

Even though they are not as likely to be noticed, don't neglect the back and sides where additional layers of dark fur create pleasing texture. Scatter dark fur sparsely into the lower reaches of the back's highlighting, then sprinkle more into the middle areas and into the area directly behind the head.

20| Paint White Details

Use a liner brush and white paint to give the inside of each ear a small cluster of curved fur lines. Add a crescent of white below each eye, underline below the angles of the nose, and paint lines along either side of the center line dividing the muzzle. Fill in the chin with white, using the tip of your brush to give the bottom a delicate fringe of splinter-sized fur that extends slightly into the dark outlines surrounding them.

21| Add More White Details

Add a bit of water to white paint to ensure it is loose enough to make long strokes that don't skip or become fuzzy. Use the tip of your liner brush to pull three crisp whiskers from the center of the muzzle on either side. Place a tiny dot of white in the upper left edge of the pupil in each eye.

22| Highlight the Paw Pads

Mix white and black to get light gray. Use it to give the small and large paw pads each a curved line of highlighting.

23 | Tint the Mane

Switch to a small flat brush. Mix a touch of Patio Brick into a drop of Sunflower Yellow and dilute with water. Use this watery mixture to add a tawny layer of transparent color to the middle areas of the mane.

24 | Finish the Muzzle

Return to your liner brush and combine black and Patio Brick to make deep brown. Scribble and dot lines along the muzzle to suggest the hair follicles there, then underline the whiskers to help them stand out and to shave them down if they got too thick.

Allow the paint to dry, then spray the rock with clear acrylic spray sealer to make the colors pop and to protect the paint.

Each lion has its own distinctive look because of the rock that was chosen and slight variations in the painting. The lioness lacks the male's dramatic mane, so adding curving lines along her body suggests rippling musculature that gives her more interest.

More zoo animals to paint

Now that you've created the lion, try your hand at painting these other big cats.

Leopard

To paint a leopard, basecoat with Pinecone Brown. Use Woodland Brown with black added to create contours and shadows. Fill in the head shape with Sunflower Yellow lightened with Cloud White and a touch of Pinecone Brown. Paint the black details and spot pattern. Fill spot centers with the same color used on the head. Use Sunflower Yellow mixed with white to create highlights and fur lines to define the haunch, head, tail and paws.

Tiger

For a tiger, basecoat the rock with Patio Brick. Darken Patio Brick with black to create shadows and contours. Use Cloud White to fill in the chest, muzzle and markings around the eyes. Paint the stripes and markings with black, then use Patio Brick lightened with Sunflower Yellow to add highlights and texture between the stripes. Use Sunflower Yellow lightened with white for more golden areas.

Cheetah

To paint a cheetah, basecoat as with a tiger, but substitute a spot pattern for the stripes. The distinctive "tear lines" help distinguish this big cat from the leopard.

Hippo Haven

Also known as River Horses, these animals may seem ungainly on land, but they are amazingly graceful and quick in water, and often spend most of their day soaking, just the curve of their broad back, the top of their head and their protruding eyes visible. While they are considered dangerous in the wild where they are capable of swamping boats and can dispatch a full-grown crocodile with a single crushing bite, it's hard to be fearful of them as they waddle about in their zoo environment, ears and tail flicking almost comically. I am especially fond of baby hippos, small replicas of their parents but often much livelier.

what you'll need

DecoArt Patio Paint in Wrought Iron Black · Patio Brick · Cloud White · Sunflower Yellow · large stiff-bristled brush · small, medium and large flats · small and medium round soft brushes · no. 1 or no. 0 liner brush · white-leaded pencil or soapstone pen · template-making supplies as listed on page 10, optional · clear acrylic spray sealer

1| Select a Rock

Almost any smooth oval-shaped rock can be transformed into a hippo. The ideal rock is a tall oval with a squared bottom, but rocks that are curved all the way around are much more common. Adding a bit of wood filler can create a stable base. The rock I'll use in this project is on the far right. It has enough height for the legs and feet and the flat base requires no additions.

2| Paint the Basecoat

Mix two parts black with one part Patio Brick and half as much white to get a deep gray with reddish undertones. Use a large stiff-bristled brush to cover the entire visible surface of the rock.

3| Sketch the Design

Once the basecoat is thoroughly dry, draw the design freehand or create a template as described on page 9. A soapstone pen or white-leaded pencil will show up best.

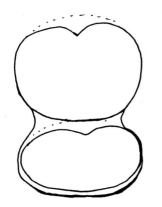

The most dominant features are the large head and muzzle. Place the muzzle oval at the most convex end of the rock. Above it place a second oval, leaving a narrow space between. Connect the two ovals with curved lines. Create a dip in the top of both ovals.

Just above the bottom of the lower oval, bring in a parallel line that makes an upward curve in the center, mirroring the dip above.

Place a round eye socket at either end of the upper oval, and add a leaf-shaped ear above both eyes, slightly indented into the oval. Add two almond-shaped nostrils to the lower oval so that they are even with the inner edge of the eye circles. In the space connecting the two ovals, add two small curved lines parallel to the connecting curves to form the corners of the mouth.

Just above the top dip of the lower oval, sketch a vertical oval that extends up from the dip to between the eyes. From the upper inside curve of each eye, sketch in a broad V shape, and give the top of the upper oval a small indent in the center. Several concentric circles surround the head shape as neck folds.

Once the head and surrounding folds are in place, the rest of this animal's layout is simple. Just behind the outer neck fold, bring down a line to represent the leading edge of the front leg, giving it a slight outward curve as you reach the bottom edge of the rock. Make a second line behind the first, starting behind the head halfway down the rock. Give this back leg line a slight crook to suggest a joint or "elbow," before bringing it down to the bottom of the rock. Place three toes along the bottom, the first just inside the back line, the next in the forward center of the foot and the third slightly past the front leg line.

Move to the back of the rock and sketch in a stocky rear leg with a more pronounced crooked back angle. Fit three toes into the end of the foot. At the rear end give the hippo rounded curves that lead to a straight tail hanging down the center.

Finally, curve a tummy line that begins just above the crook of the front leg and ends just above the center of the back leg's curve.

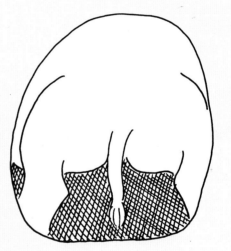

The lines around the folds in these drawings indicate shaded areas. Refer to them again when you're painting the shading.

4| Paint Out the Voids

Use black paint and a small to medium flat brush to fill in the areas around and between the legs. Paint along the lines where they extend into the body at both the front and back edge of the rear legs and the back edge of the front legs.

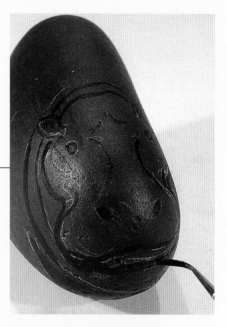

5| Outline Facial Features

Switch to a liner brush and loosen your black paint slightly with water so it flows smoothly from the brush tip. Holding your brush perpendicular to the rock surface, outline the upper head and ears. Fill in the centers of the ears. Outline the nostrils and the eyes. Define the structure of the face by painting over the inverted V between the eyes. Go over the lines for the neck folds. Outline around the muzzle and paint over the mouth line, bringing the ends around the muzzle to curve outward in the space below the eyes as shown.

6| Contour the Body

Return to your small or medium flat brush. Add enough water to black paint to create a semi-transparent wash, and shade all around the head. Skip a space then shadow immediately behind the first encircling fold. Skip another space and shadow around the outside edge of the last neck roll. Move to the back half of the front legs and shadow from the feet up to the shoulder area, leaving a narrow space of basecoat between this shadow and the back edge. Shadow the bottom third of the stomach, again leaving a line of basecoat along the edge. Curve the shadows up at either end to suggest a rotund shape. Shadow the back halves of the rear legs as you did the front legs.

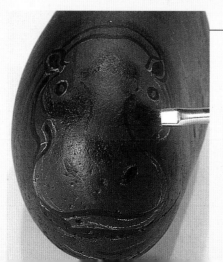

7| Add Contours to the Face

Use the same black wash to soften the inside edges of the inverted V on the forehead. Shadow along the oval above the muzzle and create a wide half-circle beneath the eyes but leave the center of the face plain.

8| Add Highlights

Mix three parts white with one part black to make a light gray, then add a touch of Patio Brick to give the gray a slight pink tone. Use a medium flat or old worn brush to pick up pigment. Wipe away excess paint and scrub on the remaining paint along the top and upper half of the hippo's body. Leave a narrow strip of basecoat uncovered along the top to suggest a spine.

Drybrushing the highlights in large areas like this is likely to produce mottled coverage, which adds desirable texture here.

9| Highlight the Head

Highlight along the top of the head above and to the edges of the inverted V shape. Also highlight the center of the elongated oval in the middle of the face. Add a curved patch below each eye. Switch to a liner brush and moisten the paint enough to create smooth lines. Go around the outsides of the ears and highlight the curves of the mouth lines to make them stand out.

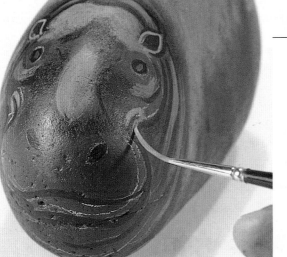

10| Add Soft Pink Touches

Start with a large drop of white paint and add in alternating increments of Sunflower Yellow and Patio Brick until you get a soft pastel pink as shown. Use a small round brush to paint the sockets surrounding the eyes. Highlight along the outside edges of the face below the ear but not quite to the mouth. Highlight the top curve of the mouth just above the gray outline painted earlier. Add this color to a short span of both neck folds just below either ear. In the center of the gray highlights at either side of the forehead, add a touch of this color with a dry brush. Place a small curving swath of highlight beside the gray highlighting down the center of the face. Paint in a solid line along the top of the muzzle. Wipe excess paint from the brush before adding a soft C shape around the top and sides of the nostrils. Finally, fill in the entire lower lip.

11| Add More Highlights on the Body

Use the same pink, but switch to a larger flat brush. Remove all but a trace of paint so that what remains must be applied with brisk scrubbing. Add a light layer of paint along the very top half of the back previously highlighted with gray, again leaving the spine uncovered. Angle your strokes back from the head so that you add both highlights and faint texture.

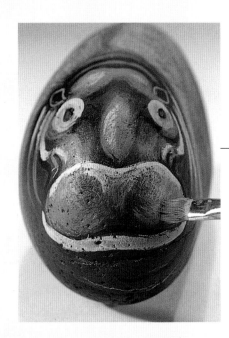

12| Deepen Flesh Tones

Mix equal parts Sunflower Yellow and Patio Brick plus a trace amount of black to get a darker, rusty colored pink. Again remove excess paint, then scrub along the dark shadows below the inverted V of the forehead and along either side of the highlighted center of the face. Add a swath of color along the contour of the upper curve of the mouth on both sides of the head. Darken the flesh tone folds and the upper curve of the face just below the ears. Finally, lightly fill the muzzle below the nostrils, leaving the center of the muzzle plain.

13| Paint Eye Details

Use Patio Brick lightened with just a touch of Sunflower Yellow to fill in the eye circles. Use a liner brush and go around the edges as needed to create smooth outlines. Switch to plain Patio Brick and add narrow half-circles both above and below the eyes without allowing ends to touch.

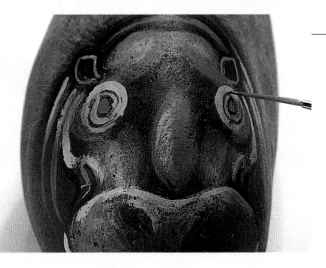

14| Add Dots to Muzzle

While you have Patio Brick on the tip of your liner brush, add a few dots to each side of the muzzle.

15| Enhance Details With Pale Gray

Mix up four parts white and one part black to make a very light gray. Use the tip of your liner brush to go around the edges of the head, across the top and along the sides of the muzzle, accentuating the figure-eight shape. Go around the outside openings of the nostrils. Sprinkle dots of this pale gray among the dots previously painted on the muzzle.

16| Detail the Body

Outline around the legs and along the tummy with the light gray. Outline the tail and the rounded rump between the tail and back leg on either side.

17| Detail the Neck Folds

Go over the edges of all the neck folds. I added another partial fold to fill in extra space between the last neck fold and the front leg.

18| Paint the Toenails

Hippos, like elephants, have broad, rounded toenails rather than actual toes. Use a small to medium round brush and the same light gray paint to fill in the toenails for each foot. Make them ovals that come to a point at the tips. Once they are all painted, go back with plain white and give each nail a curved top line of highlighting.

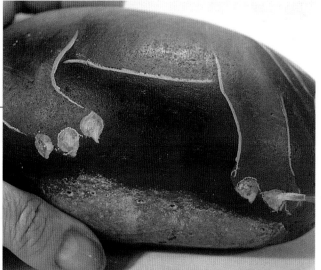

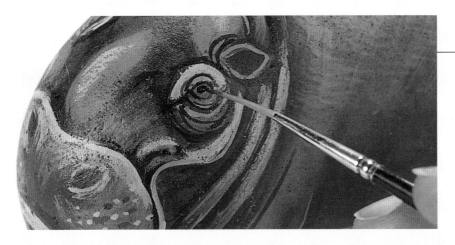

19| Add More Details to the Ears and Eyes

Use a liner brush and black paint to make two thin curving lines like wrinkles above each ear. Paint around the outside edges of the eye sockets. Add thin curved lines to the eyes, both above and below, and add a second thin line below the first one under the eye to emphasize the lines there. Add small pupils to the center of each eye.

20| Add Black Details

Add tiny dots of black to the left side of every gray dot on the muzzle. Use the tip of your liner brush to place sparse, somewhat random sets of tiny lines on the hippo's back and shoulders parallel to the spine.

21| Finish the Body

Use black paint to make sure that the curve of the haunch and the upper halves of the front legs are clearly delineated so that they stand out from the body.

Add white to create a light gray and use it to further define the edges of the front and back legs. Using a liner brush, sprinkle gray texture lines along the midsection of the hippo's sides and flanks. These light lines stand out against the dark hippo skin as the dark lines did against previously highlighted areas.

22| Add Gleam

Add a tiny dot of white in each eye to provide the spark of life. Allow the paint to dry, then spray the rock with clear acrylic spray sealer to make the colors pop and to protect the paint.

Happy hippos all in a row! The rock on the left was too flat, so I added pieces of gravel for legs. To do this, glue gravel with a flat end to the rock and allow to set. Then use a small amount of wood filler to cover the joints. Filler tends to soften glue temporarily, so apply just enough to cover the cracks first and let it harden before using additional filler to smooth the surface and sculpt splayed feet. The tip of a paintbrush handle can make a good tool for smoothing and shaping filler. Once painted, it's hard to tell the additions from the natural rock.

More zoo animals to paint

Creating a rhinoceros is easy by making a few modifications to the hippo instructions and adding a wood filler horn.

Rhinos

To paint a rhino, start with a light gray basecoat and use heavy lines to suggest the leathery armor-plated skin. Much of the detail, including the eyes, neck folds and toes, is painted similarly to the hippo.

I used wood filler to build up the horns, but bits of angular gravel can also be glued on and blended in with filler.

Polar Bear's Winter Home

The polar bear body is almost sculptural. A streamlined head and relatively bulky hindquarters combine to give them something of a pear shape. Rarely is their coat pure white. Instead, subtle undertones range from the palest of ivory or gray to deep rusty red or golden hues.

I recently watched a polar bear swim laps in a glass-walled tank before an appreciative audience at the Indianapolis Zoo. It was amazing to witness this huge animal swimming with such athletic grace, stopping and turning with perfect precision before launching himself in the opposite direction. It is moments like this that keep me seeking out new zoos whenever I travel.

what you'll need

DecoArt Patio Paint in Pinecone Brown · Wrought Iron Black · Cloud White · Sunflower Yellow, optional · small and large stiff-bristled flat brushes · medium and small round or flat brushes · no. 0 or no. 1 liner brush · customized fur brush, rake or comb brush, optional · pencil · template-making supplies, listed on page 10, optional · clear acrylic spray sealer

1| Select Your Rock

A wide range of rock shapes can be painted as polar bears. A crouching or resting bear with its head turned back in profile is one of the easier poses. With practice you may see other possibilities, like mother/cub combinations, bears standing on all fours or even rearing up on their hind legs. For this project, choose a rock with a flat bottom and a rounded, rather humped top side. Sloping or rounded tops will work and so will rocks with more boxy shapes so long as there are no sharp angles. The rock I chose is on the left, a smooth oval with one slightly smaller end.

2| Paint the Basecoat

Although the basecoat color will be almost completely covered by layers of fur, it sets the tone by providing contrast that allows the lighter fur strokes to stand out. I prefer the look of warmer undertones so I used straight Pinecone Brown. You can make your basecoat solid gray or gray blended with Pinecone Brown or choose a more golden color by mixing Sunflower Yellow and Pinecone Brown. Apply the basecoat with a large stiff-bristled flat brush, covering all but the very bottom of the rock. Let dry.

3| Draw or Transfer the Pattern

Because this pose is relatively simple, you may prefer to sketch on the guidelines freehand. If not, create a template of the head shape, adjusting the size to fit your rock. (See page 9 for template instructions.) My bear's head measures 3 inches (7cm) from nose to the tip of the larger ear, while the entire rock is about 8 inches (20cm) long.

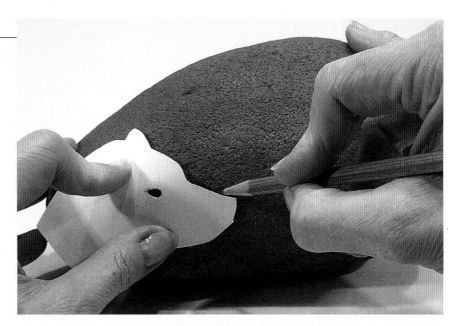

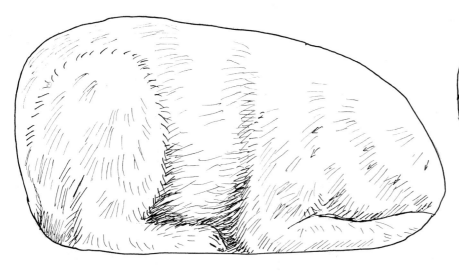

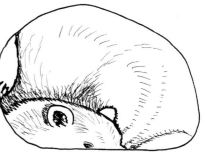

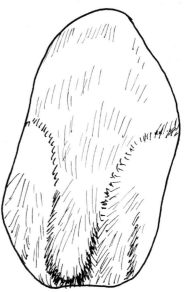

Using these sketches as a guide, add a rounded haunch at the other end that is about the same diameter as the length of the head. Draw an elongated oval foreleg and rounded paw, with the joint or elbow having a right angle that is overlapped by the tip of the bear's muzzle and nose. Extend a rear foot from the lower inside edge of the haunch, and indicate the upper leg with a short vertical line extending into the center of the haunch. Add a rear leg to the backside of the rock as well as a second front paw and foreleg with the upper leg coming up at a right angle.

These drawings also serve as your fur direction guides. Refer to them again when you're painting the fur so that your polar bear's fur will look more natural.

4 | Establish Contours

Combine equal parts Pinecone Brown and black to get a dark color that is less harsh than straight black. Use a small, stiff-bristled brush to darken the space between the head and the front paw and foreleg, the space between the front leg and the rear paw, and the triangle of shadow at the crook of the rear paw and haunch. Fill in the center of the near ear and outline around both ears. Outline the shape of the head, using less paint on your brush so that these strokes look soft. Fill in the muzzle area (but not the chin) with the same soft application and run a narrow line up along the center of the muzzle to the forehead.

5 | Continue to Paint Contours

Establish the cleft of shadow that defines the upper leg on both the front and back sides. Do the same around the curve of the haunch front and back. Lightly suggest a short curve of shadow in the bear's upper midsection, and add shadows to the area between the tail and the vertical line that define the back of the rear leg. Apply shadows to the same areas on the backside as well. On the front end, darken the space between the two front paws. At the tail end, darken the U-shaped shadow that defines the blunt, stubby tail.

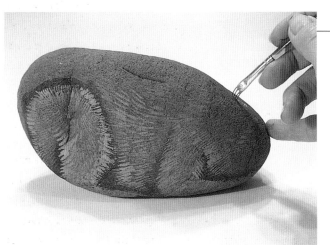

6 | Add Fur to the Back

Begin with the same mix of black and Pinecone Brown, then add increments of white until you get a discernably lighter shade of gray. You can apply the undercoat fur with a liner brush, a rake or comb brush, or a small customized flat brush (see page 9). Regardless of which brush is used, loosen the paint with enough water to allow it to go on in smooth, unbroken lines. Begin in the back where your practice strokes will not be as apparent. Paint fur lines heaviest where the tips slightly overlap any shadowed areas, but leave most of the shadowing uncovered. Use the fur directional guide on page 41 for help with placing lines for the most natural look. Paint the haunch and back leg, then fill in the front leg and paw on this side. The fur in the midsection can be looser and less dense.

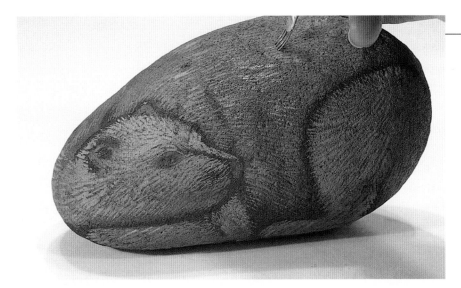

7 | Add Fur to Front of Bear

On the front side, apply gray fur lines to the haunch first. Paint splinter strokes (dense, closely spaced strokes) around the edges of the haunch and hind leg and on the head and foreleg. Fill in the rest of these areas with similar strokes. Paint fur on the face, following the fur direction guide. Again make the fur on the body less dense.

8 | Paint Layers of White Fur

Use the same brush to apply a full coat of pure white fur lines to the bear. Add water to your paint so that it flows easily off the bristles. Make sets of white fur lines densest in the highlight areas, which are around the outside edge of the rear haunch and the upper edge of the rear foot, along the back side of the upper foreleg and the top of the lower foreleg and paw. Note that I left a hint of dark crease showing at the angle where the upper and lower foreleg meet. I also made a heavy fringe along the back edge of the leg, but was careful to leave a trace of the dark shadowing in place to keep the various elements clearly separate and defined.

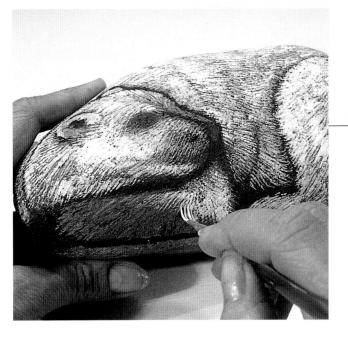

9 | Add White to Front of Bear

Use your liner brush to outline around the edges of the outer ear and to fill in the inner or back ear with solid white. Give the outer ear a fringe of fur along the inner edges. When detailing the head, consult the fur direction guide and apply fur lines so heavily that they are almost solid along the very top of the head and in the jowl area below and between the eye and ear. Also fill in the chin with white fur so that it creates a solid line with a fringed bottom edge. Continue to fill in the areas with fur, tilting your rock to add white fur details to lower areas.

10| Paint Details With Black

Use pure black and your liner brush to create a row of three curved lines along the tips of the front paws to delineate the toes. Add small triangular claws to the paws between the toe lines. Fill in the eye with black, keeping it small enough to avoid a cartoonish look. Paint a dark line for the mouth and fill in the nose leather.

11| Create Subtle Shading

Use a soft-bristled flat or round brush to apply tints to give your polar bear a warm, golden tone. I used Pinecone Brown mixed with enough water to make it transparent. You can also tint with a combination of Pinecone Brown and Sunflower Yellow for a more golden tone or, for a cooler tone, mix gray with a touch of Sunflower Yellow. If you aren't sure which you'd prefer, experiment on the backside of the rock, keeping a paper towel handy to pat away excess paint or pick up all the paint.

The key to success is keeping the wash understated while allowing it to deepen and enrich the shadows and recesses of the animal. Avoid applying tints to any of the pure white areas, instead concentrating them beside or behind such areas to increase contrast. Specifically, tint around the edges of the face and head, around the haunch and along the top of the front leg where it is overshadowed by the head shape. Add a swath of tint to the very back of the rear leg behind the crease there. After tints are applied, use your fingertip or the corner of a paper towel to blend or soften any sharp edges.

12 | Paint Soft White Highlights

Rinse your brush and dilute white paint with enough water to make the paint semi-transparent. You can test the consistency by making test strokes on newsprint. The paint should be thick enough to whiten the print yet thin enough to easily read the type. Keep a paper towel handy to dab away excess pigment.

Use this white wash to soften the gray undercoat showing between the fur lines in areas that need to be very white. These areas include the tops of the shoulders and along the back between the shadowy creases and the tops of both haunches. If needed, tint the top of the head and the lightest area along the cheek below the eye and running back to just below the ear. If the consistency of your paint is right, you will soften the contrasting gray without covering it completely so that the texture of fur is still visible, while the overall appearance of the animal is noticeably lightened.

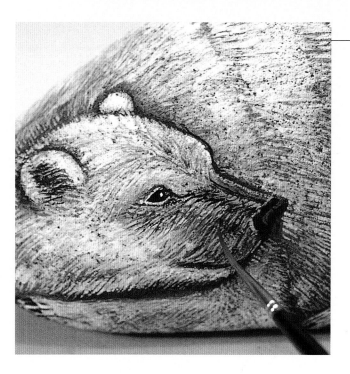

13 | Add Fine Details

Use the tip of the liner brush to add a narrow, defining line of white paint along the top line of the muzzle from just behind the nose leather back to the rounded bump on the forehead over the second, unseen eye. Outline the eye just inside the edges, leaving a narrow band of dark around the outside to set it off. Add a gleam to the eye with a dot of white.

Next stroke on a row of very short, slanted lines along the outside edge of the dark line up the center of the muzzle. Make a second row of longer strokes just beyond that row leaving a narrow edge of dark in between. Sprinkle a few more white lines in the center of the muzzle and use a narrow outline to define the top of the mouth line. A narrow line of white around the base of the nose leather will also set it off.

Mix a tiny amount of black into your white paint to get a medium gray and use this to give the nose a soft gleam. With black on the liner brush, paint a line between the rows of fur on the muzzle. Add a row of fur from the eye to the nose leather and a few additional fur lines in the center of the ear and on the muzzle.

14| Add Finishing Touches With Gray

Completing your polar bear at this point is an exercise in spotting both the areas that need a little more dark detail or definition and those that need lighter touches. Begin by mixing white with black to get a deep shade of gray. Add enough water to allow you to make very narrow, crisp lines. With your liner brush, make very spare accents of fur in areas that need rebalancing.

On my rock, the lower half of the haunches became a bit too light when I was white washing. Since this area should be somewhat shadowed, I sprinkled a few dark fur lines around the bottom and along the side a bit back from the edge. I added a few dark lines to the inside crook of the front leg, and a few more along the swath of shadow below the cheek area. On your rock you may see other areas that need retouching or where fur texture has been lost. A few narrow lines will often correct such spots.

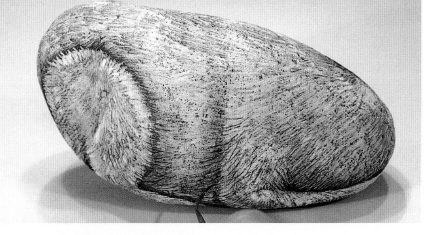

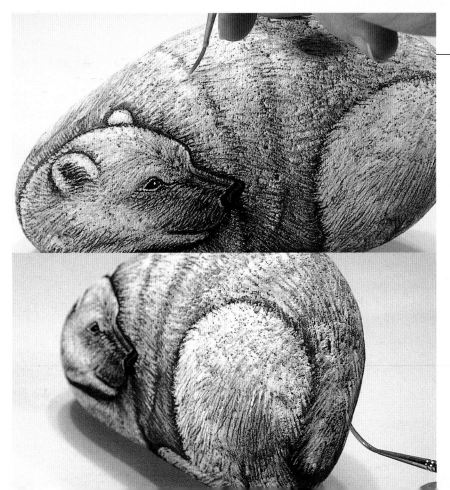

15| Add Finishing Touches With White

Continue to rebalance as you switch to white paint, now looking for areas where the white washing could use strengthening. These areas are likely to vary, so it's a chance to develop your "artist's eye" by determining where more white details are needed. On the backside of my rock I added more white fur to the edge along the back of the upper leg and in the center of the midsection. I gave the tail a fringe of white fur to balance out the brown tint there. The shoulder area behind the head at the far end of the rock is another area that frequently needs more attention. Allow the paint to dry, they spray the rock with clear acrylic sealer to heighten the colors and protect the paint.

Each of these polar bears is posed in a way that best suits the surface. If your rock has a lot of height, try making a mother and cub rock like I did on the right.

More zoo animals to paint

Much of what you learned when painting the polar bear can be applied to these animals as well. Give them a try too!

Black Bear

To paint a black bear, cover the entire rock with a basecoat of black. When dry, use a white-leaded pencil to sketch on the head, the front legs and paws and the back haunches. Use medium to light shades of gray to create fur lines that highlight the tops and sides of the head and the sides of the front legs and the tops of the haunches. Mix Summer Sky Blue with a touch of black and water it down to a wash you can use to blend the edges of the highlights and soften them. Mix Sunflower Yellow with a small amount of white and a touch of black and use this to create a contrasting muzzle area.

Koala

To paint a koala, basecoat the surface in dark brown, and outline the head and legs with black. Paint shades of white and tan splinter strokes around the features and use these same colors to fill out the fur and give the coat its plush, flecked look.

Primate Place

The primate exhibits are always at the top of my list of must-see animals at any zoo. It is intriguing to watch these creatures and to note how closely their gestures and interactions resemble those of humans. The more intelligent the animals, the more interesting they are to observe, and all the great apes offer an endless array of fascinating behaviors. Whether it's the carefree play of youngsters, the social grooming of adults or the calmly astute gaze of the alpha male looking back at me, I come away with a renewed respect for the dignity of these truly magnificent beings.

A young chimp's winsome expression is hard to resist, yet this appealing primate is surprisingly easy to paint and requires only a few colors.

what you'll need

DecoArt Patio Paint in Wrought Iron Black · Cloud White · Patio Brick · Antique Mum · Geranium Red · large, medium and small stiff-bristled flat brushes · small soft round brush · no. 0 or no. 1 liner brush · graphite pencil or soapstone pen · wood filler, optional · template-making supplies, listed on page 10, optional · clear acrylic spray sealer

1 | Select a Rock

The best rock for this project has a flat base and an upright shape that tapers to a rounded top. Chimps can be painted in just about any size, but smaller rocks requiring finer details may prove more challenging than larger ones. If your rock will not stand or is wobbly, adding wood filler to an uneven base can correct this.

2 | Paint the Basecoat

Mix equal parts white and black to get a medium shade of gray. Add enough Patio Brick to warm up the gray slightly. Use a large stiff-bristled flat brush to cover all the exposed areas of your rock and let dry.

3 | Sketch the Design

Chimp rocks come in a variety of sizes and shapes, so it may be easiest to create a template of the head (see page 9 for instructions), enlarging the size as needed. Once the head is positioned and outlined, sketch on the rest of the animal freehand. The most common mistake with this animal is to oversize the head. On my rock the head (as measured from chin to crown) takes up about one-third of the height of the rock.

To sketch the chimp's face on your own, begin with a heart. Draw a circle that intersects the bottom two-thirds of the heart.

Connect the heart and circle with a line for the side of the face. Draw the eyes, nostrils and mouth, keeping them parallel. Add ears.

These drawings are patterns as well as fur direction guides. Refer to them as you paint so that your chimp's fur will look natural.

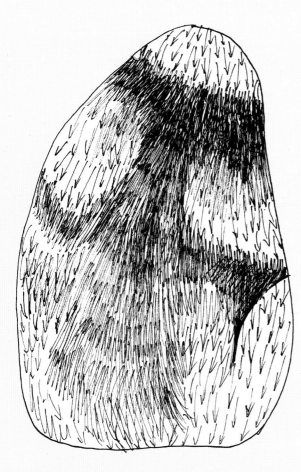

Here I used a regular graphite pencil to sketch the chimp. If your basecoat is darker, you could use a soapstone pen or white-leaded pencil.

4 | Paint Shadows to Create Contours

Use a small stiff-bristled brush and black paint to create the illusion of dimension that helps establish the features and makes them stand out. Drybrush along and below the chin with black, extending it down over the chest to the tops of the arms. Paint a dark line around the bottom edges of both arms to define them, and do the same around the drawn-up legs before filling in the space between them, below the hand, with solid black. Also fill in the triangular spaces on the sides where the elbows meet the thighs, and extend a dark curving line at each hip to suggest a crease there. Wipe excess paint from your brush and blend outward from deepest shadows to soften harsh edges.

5 | Continue Contours on Back

On the head, surround the ears with a narrower black border that widens like a collar to separate the head and back. Create a wide spine extending from the back of the head toward the base of the rock. Soften this spine line by scrubbing out along the edges with a dry brush. A little less than halfway down from the top of the rock, use straight black paint to suggest a pair of shoulder blades creating solid shadows beneath them in a rounded W-shape. Drop down and echo these curved shadows with a lower set. At the bottom of the rock darken the base from hip to hip. Refer to the fur direction guide on page 51 for placement of these dark areas.

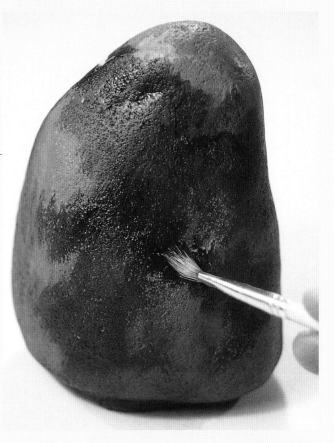

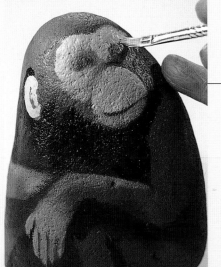

6 | Fill in With Peach

Begin with a small puddle of Antique Mum and add tiny increments of Geranium Red until you get a pale peach color. Use a small round brush to paint in the fingers and toes. Remove excess paint from the brush before scrubbing subtle traces along the top line of both forearms. Pick up more paint to fill in the round ear on one side and the teardrop-shaped portion of the other ear. Paint the face, leaving a narrow space separating the muzzle from the upper face. Go carefully around the eye openings and mouth line.

7 | Detail the Features

With a liner brush, outline the eyes shapes with black thinned with just enough water to ensure the paint will flow easily off the tip of your brush. Mix a small amount of black into Patio Brick to get a deep brown color and add water to thin in the same way. Because the head is turned, the eyes, nose and mouth should be on parallel planes. Carefully paint in the upper lip, tipping up the ends and making a subtle rise near the right side, where the center would be with the head turned. Make a thicker but shorter lower lip line below. Paint two small, slanted nostrils, centered in the face just below the top of the muzzle. Check for symmetry by holding a pencil even with the eyes, nose and mouth. All three should remain parallel.

8 | Contour and Shadow the Skin

Add small amounts of Patio Brick and Geranium Red to the peach to get a deep rusty red color. With the liner, use this to a create a solid half-circle of shadow above each eye that reach midway into the forehead and create the suggestion of a brow above. The inside edge of each half-circle should taper to a point just south of the eye, forming a shallow bridge above the nose. Paint a small V-shaped shadow over the nostrils. Paint a narrow line to define the top of the muzzle and delicate wrinkle lines in the muzzle above the mouth, keeping them soft and subtle.

Make a row of short strokes like hair roots along the border between the forehead and dark crown to softly integrate those two areas. Also shadow the inside of the ear (see detail below) and use this deeper color to add wrinkles and joint lines at the knuckles of the hand and along the toes.

Finally use the tip of your brush to add several delicate half-circles below each eye, fanning them out from the inside corners.

Ear Detail

To create the ear, paint it with peach (step 6). Paint the contours of the ear with a deep rusty red (step 8). Highlight the outer rim and inner curves with Antique Mum (step 10) and outline these edges with a mix of Patio Brick and black (step 11).

9 | Paint Fur Layers

Rinse your liner brush and mix a small amount of water into black paint to get a consistency loose enough to create thin yet distinct lines. Hold your brush tip nearly perpendicular to the rock surface and stroke on the fur. Keep the lines sparse enough to allow the basecoat color to show through and even sparser on the arms over the peach color. Stroke on a few fur lines that extend past the wrist but stop well before reaching the tops of the fingers. When painting the head and hairline, it may be helpful to turn the rock around and pull the strokes toward yourself, anchoring the "roots" along the top of the forehead to create a second layer of fringe there. Work around the sides of the face, adding fur to the small wedges formed between the bottoms of the ears and the sides of the muzzle. Keep the fur sparse enough to let the lighter color below show through. Refer to the fur direction guide on page 51 as needed.

10 | Detail the Face

Still using the liner brush, fill in the eye circles with Patio Brick darkened slightly with a touch of black. Rinse and paint in two small round pupils with black paint.

Switch to straight Antique Mum to highlight the face. With a dry stubby brush, softly highlight along the forehead just above the brows. Then highlight the upper and lower eyelids with the liner and thinner paint. Lighten the top and sides of the nostrils and the spaces between the red half-circles below the eyes. Add narrow highlights along the wrinkle lines in the muzzle to give them more dimension. Highlight the outside rim and inner curves of the ear as well (part of the ear detail on page 53). Add a fringe of light whiskers to the chin. Emphasize the mouth with a highlight along the top of the upper lip.

11 | Add Final Touches to Face and Hands

Using a dark mix of Patio Brick and black, add a row of short, slanted strokes that indicate two skimpy eyebrows. Add dark lines around the outsides of the upper and lower eyelids to clearly define them. Outline the curves of the ear as well. To warm the eyes, add a narrow half-circle of straight Patio Brick to the bottom curve of each iris.

With black on the liner, stroke on a few very delicate eyelashes, slanting them in the direction the head is turned.

Finish detailing the hand and feet, using a dark mix of Patio Brick and black to emphasize knuckle wrinkles and to add nails to all the fingers and toes.

12 | Finish the Fur

Mix Antique Mum and a small amount of black to get a warm light gray for fur highlights. Add fur lines to the very top of the head and around the face. Paint lines to set off the top curve of the shoulders. Scatter fur lines in the center of the dark chest area to bring this area forward slightly, but leave dark margins in place to keep the chest defined. Highlight the tops of the arms and the edges of the legs as well.

13 | Finish the Eyes

Dot a speck of white into the center of each pupil and watch how your chimp suddenly seems to be staring back at you!

Allow the paint to dry, then spray a light coating of clear acrylic sealer to seal the piece and heighten the colors.

This little chimp's large, bright eyes make him absolutely adorable. He's posed in a way that takes advantage of the roundness of the rock I used.

Moᵣe zoo animals to paint

Monkeys are absolutely fascinating to watch at the zoo, and they're a lot of fun to paint. Here are a few more ideas for painting primates.

Gorillas

For a gorilla, basecoat the entire visible surface of the rock with solid black. Mix white and black to make gray for the facial features and fur.

Add Tango Blue in small increments to black paint and add water to create a watery wash. Use it to tone down the gray areas, leaving areas of these fur lines uncovered as the strongest highlights.

Orangutans

To paint an orangutan, use black softened with Patio Brick for the basecoat. Layer on fur with combinations of Patio Brick, Sunflower Yellow and Tiger Lily Orange. Use the same skin tones that you mixed for the chimp.

Baboon Pair

To paint these baboons, basecoat with a mix of Patio Brick and black to create a deep brown. Sketch on the mother with a white-leaded pencil. I used wood filler to build up the ears slightly. Tuck the baby below so that it sits no higher than halfway up the rock. Use black paint to deepen the contours and heighten contrasts. With a mixture of white and Sunflower Yellow outline the features with splinter strokes, then layer on the remaining fur. When dry, use a wash of Sunflower Yellow to heighten the golden colors on the shoulders. Darken with a mix of black and Patio Brick and add water to create a wash. Use this wash to soften the fur in the more shadowed areas. Paint the baby's face with a mixture of Sunflower Yellow and white plus a hint of Geranium Red. Add more white for highlights and Patio Brick for shadows.

Golden Lion Tamarin

This small primate is remarkable for its vividly golden coloring as well as its expressive face. Begin by covering the rock with Patio Brick. Once you've sketched on the outlines, use black paint to establish the shadows and contours that give the animal added dimension. Mix Sunshine Yellow with a small amount of Patio Brick and use this golden color to layer on long fur lines until the piece is well covered. Add more yellow to the mix and lighten the tops of the head, arms and tail. Use a mix with more Patio Brick added to lightly sprinkle darker fur along the lower area of these same features. For the face, mix a very pale gray and add a touch of both red and Sunflower Yellow.

Toucan Jungle

Tropical toucans, with their wildly outsized bills and flamboyant coloring, make an exotic addition to any rock zoo. Toucans and their close relatives, the hornbills, come in a rainbow of colorations and beak patterns. Like parrots, they have a compact, nearly neckless shape that makes them fairly easy to fit onto rocks.

what you'll need

DecoArt Patio Paints in Wrought Iron Black · Cloud White · Sunshine Yellow · Tiger Lily Orange · Citrus Green · Tango Blue · Daisy Cream · soapstone pen or regular graphite pencil · small and medium stiff-bristled flat brushes · small and medium soft round and flat brushes · ⅜ inch (10mm) or smaller angular shader brush · no. 0 or no. 1 liner brush · template-making supplies, listed on page 10, optional · wood filler, optional · clear acrylic spray sealer

1| Select a Rock

The best rocks on which to paint a toucan stand up tall on a flat base. They can be leveled to stand by adding wood filler. If your rock has one more angular side, or an area that bows out, consider placing the beak there.

Larger rocks make more dramatic pieces, but the one I chose is a little over 5 inches (13cm) tall with a neatly rounded top and smoothly sloping sides. Though not very tall, the shape of this rock seemed to suggest the flared-out back side of the bird's tail end. It has only a small curve, so making the beak look slightly turned will help show its distinctive shape.

2| Sketch the Design

Use a graphite pencil or soapstone pen to sketch the design or make a template of it as described on page 9. This design must begin with the beak shape because all other elements are dictated by its placement. Not only is the toucan's bill hugely oversized, but the upper beak also has a distinctive curve. To show it, I turned the beak on my bird just slightly to one side so that both the top half and the smaller, straighter bottom half would be visible. Start the beak very near the top of the rock, curving it down toward the base. On this rock the beak measures almost 4 inches (10cm), or four-fifths of the total height of the rock. For taller rocks, the percentage may be slightly less, but you would never want the beak to be less than two-thirds of the rock's height. If your rock has a more pronounced curve than mine does, there may be no need to skew the beak sideways.

The rest of the design consists of the one-piece facemask and connected bib that ends just above the beak tip, the eyes and the two wing shapes. To give your bird a built-in perch, draw in a narrow branch just above the base running sideways until it curves out of sight. Add two bird feet that overlap the branch below the tip of the beak.

Refer to these drawings as you're painting your toucan for guidance on feather direction.

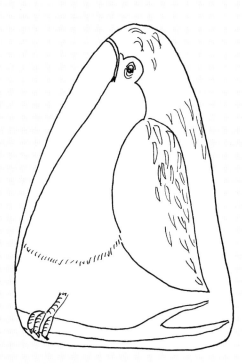

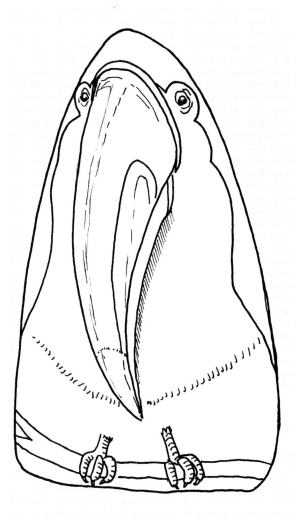

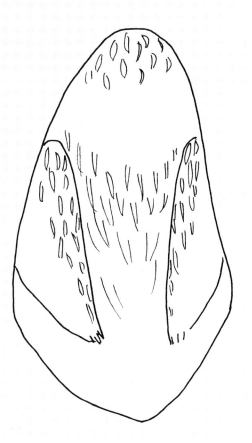

3| Paint the Black Areas

Use a medium, stiff-bristled brush and black to cover the rock, excluding the mask, bib, beak, eyes and the branch. Coverage needs to be solid, so if your rock surface is rough, work the paint into all the nooks and crannies. The contoured edges of the mask and bib should be smooth, but the line along the bottom of the bib should have a bit of texture.

4| Paint the Beak

Rinse your brush well before covering the beak with Citrus Green. Leave a narrow band along the top curve of the beak uncovered for now. A second coat may be needed if your rock is dark. If you are concerned about losing the guideline for the lower beak, simply paint right alongside the line, leaving it uncovered.

5| Paint the Mask and Bib

Use Sunshine Yellow to cover the mask and fill in the bib area, leaving only the eye spaces uncovered. Along the bottom of the bib, feather the tips of your strokes out into the area you left textured earlier. Everywhere else the edges of these yellow areas should be as smooth as possible. If you are painting on a dark or very smooth stone, a second coat of yellow may be necessary.

6| Paint Circles Around the Eyes

Switch to a liner brush and use Citrus Green to create several small concentric circles around each eye. You may need to add a drop of water to help the paint go on smoothly.

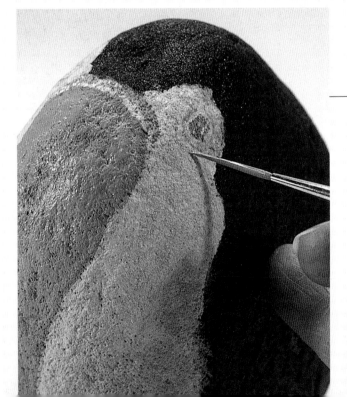

7| Add Highlights to the Beak

Switch to a small or medium round or flat brush to give the beak a streak of Sunshine Yellow highlighting from the top curve down the center of the beak, tapering it off near the tip. Go along the bottom edge of the upper beak with a narrow line of highlighting. Near the top of the upper beak, add a large oval spot with a tapering end.

8| Highlight the Wings and Back

Mix two parts white with one part black and slightly less than one part Tango Blue to make a bluish-gray. Use a medium-sized angular or flat brush to pick up paint, wiping away much of it for drybrushing. Begin at the top of the head, just behind the mask around the eyes, applying a cluster of strokes that fan out backwards. Skip down to the center of the back and add more strokes of highlighting there.

A wide band of black should remain between the back highlights and the tops of the wings, so use a smaller brush to paint in an outline of the wing shapes to clearly establish them. The back highlights can be stroked on in several overlapping layers that reach nearly to the back edge of the rock.

On the wings, concentrate your drybrushed strokes along the top edges, and add several offset rows of strokes to suggest the texture of slanting wing feathers.

9| Add a Tail

Use the same bluish-gray paint and a liner brush to paint a tail at the very bottom of the back of the bird. The tail is a square shape with an inverted V split in the center.

10| Paint the Branch

The original color of my rock was close to the pale beige I wanted for the branch that forms the toucan's perch. Make the color by mixing small increments of black into a larger puddle of Daisy Cream. Paint the branch with a small flat brush. Use a liner brush to paint around the feet and between the toes.

Add more black to the mixture and run a line of shadowing just above the bottom edge of the branch.

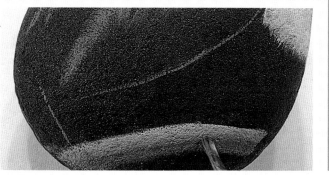

11| Sharpen the Details

Fill in the two eyes with the tip of your liner brush and black paint.

Paint in the band along the top of the beak solid black, tapering the end on the side the beak is turned toward. On the other side, bring the end down until it's even with the edge of the upper beak. Run a black line down between the upper and lower beaks, starting out heavier but narrowing the line as it goes down. Narrowly outline around the top and bottom edges of the entire beak to make it stand out clearly. At the corner of the band around the top of the beak, extend a small curving line.

12| Detail the Feather Highlights

Use your liner brush and black paint to add narrow layers of long lines that break up the larger gray highlights on the head, back and wings. These fine lines may curve in various directions, but they should follow the overall direction of the highlights. Avoid the very top edge of highlighting to preserve maximum contrast there.

13| Detail the Eyes

Mix a trace amount of black into a drop of Citrus Green and use the resulting greenish-gray color to play up the curves along the bottom halves of the circles surrounding the eyes.

14| Paint the Beak Tip

Mix small increments of black into a small puddle of Tiger Lily Orange to make a rusty brown color. Use your liner brush to fill in the tip of the beak, giving the top a pronounced inward curve. Don't cover up the yellow edges around the beak tip. On the bottom beak, start the brown area a little lower down, curving the top so the inner edge comes up nearly level with that of the top beak.

15| Add Beak Stripes

Use the same rusty brown color to add four small crescents along the bottom edge of the upper beak. Add a longer row of smaller and less curved V-shaped markings to the top line of the lower beak, offsetting them slightly so that they don't line up evenly with the crescents above.

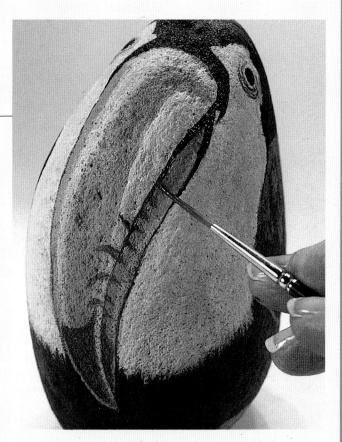

16| Add Dark Fringe

With the same rusty color used on the beak, make a border of short, delicate lines along the bottom edge of the toucan's bib.

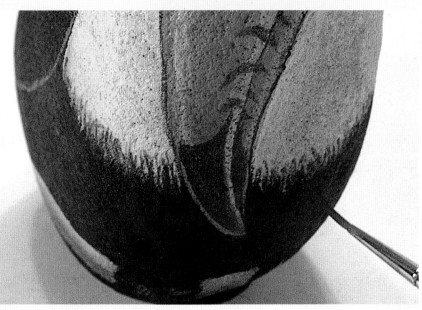

17| Shadow Beneath the Beak

A line of shadowing will add to the illusion that the beak is actually standing out from the body. Use a small stiff-bristled flat, adding increments of black paint to a drop of Citrus Green until you have an olive-drab shade of gray-green. Remove excess pigment from the brush and scrub this color along the side of the beak. Make the line of shadow narrow at the top, gradually widening it as you move down to the bottom of the bib.

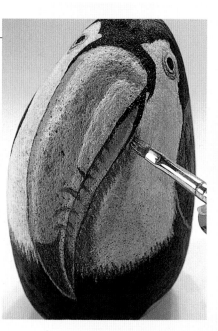

18| Add Orange Touches

Select a small round or flat brush and use Tiger Lily Orange to brighten the center of the beak's yellow spot, leaving an edge of yellow showing along the top. Paint the edges of the beak tip orange, too. Use either the tip of that same brush or a liner brush to add a row of orange fringe right over the top of the darker fringe along the bottom of the bib.

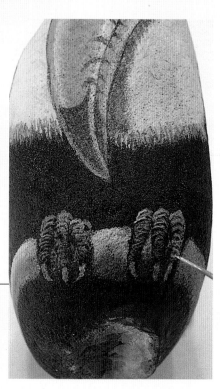

19| Detail the Feet

Mix white with a small amount of black to get a medium gray. Use your liner brush to add a small, curved nail to each toe. Move up from the nail and fill each toe with a row of closely spaced horizontal lines, curving them to indicate dimension. Make these "scaly" lines heavier and closer together toward the top of each toe. Leave black edges in place so the toes remain separate.

20| Add Final Touch

A single dot of white in the center of each eye gives this bird a bright and inquisitive stare.

Allow the paint to dry, then spray the rock with clear acrylic sealer to heighten the colors and protect the paint.

Make a whole flock of these colorful birds to add a tropical flare to any décor! Note how the beak for each of these birds is placed based on the features of the rock it's painted on.

More zoo animals to paint

The feather work on this owl is more like fur compared to the feathers on the toucan. The long, curved feather lines make the owl look fluffy and warm.

Watchful Owl

To paint this owl, begin with a white basecoat, then use Patio Brick darkened with black to add the breast feathers. On the back and sides, use solid deep brown to paint the wings, back and tail feathers. Use straight black to define the shape of the head and the features, then use white to create the delicate patterns on the head and around the neck.

Zebra Plains

The bold contrast of black against white gives the zebra one of the most starkly dramatic color combinations possible. The stripe pattern can be challenging, but once the guidelines are in place, a minimum of fur details makes this zebra a fairly easy animal to paint. Zebras are muscular and compact, built more like sturdy ponies than horses. Once you've mastered this resting pose, you may want to try augmenting your rocks to create a whole herd of these wonderful animals in a variety of lifelike poses.

what you'll need

DecoArt Patio Paint in Cloud White · Wrought Iron Black · Daisy Cream · Patio Brick · Sunflower Yellow · large, stiff-bristled flat brush · small and medium soft flat brushes · small round and small shader brushes · no. 0 or no. 1 liner brush · template-making supplies, listed on page 10, optional · waxed paper and black permanent marker, optional · clear acrylic spray sealer

1| Select A Rock

Look for a rock with an oval shape and flat bottom. It should be wide enough to suggest the bulk of this sturdy creature and tall enough to fit the head and pricked up ears. If you find a rock with an uneven top that suggests a raised head, that's a plus, but it's not necessary. One slightly squared off end can work well for the chest and neck, but the end for the hindquarters needs to be rounded. For this project I chose the center rock.

2| Paint the Basecoat

Use a large stiff-bristled flat brush to cover the rock surface with white. Paint down to the base so that no plain rock is visible.

3| Sketch the Design

Start with positioning the head shape. If you are comfortable with your drawing skills, use the step-by-step guide. Otherwise, create a template from the patterns provided, as described on page 9, adjusting the size to fit your rock. Whichever method you use, the head should be placed as high on the rock as it can go without having the ears curve out of view.

To sketch the zebra head, begin with a large circle for the head and a smaller one for the muzzle. Draw neck lines coming off of the head.

Sketch the ears with their bases inside the circle for the head. Draw the eyes and nostrils, keeping them parallel to the ears.

Once the head is in place, tuck the folded front leg below it near the end of the rock. Add the round back haunch, slightly flattening the inside curve. Sketch in a crooked back leg whose outside edge bisects the bottom of the haunch. Tilting the midsection of the leg up slightly allows you to gracefully angle the ankle joint down to the hoof. Do the same with the back leg on the other side of the rock, and tuck in another folded front leg.

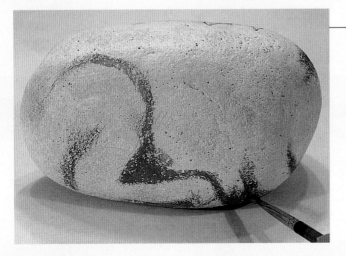

4| Paint the Shadows

While some animals require dark shadows to establish contours, a zebra, with its stripe pattern, requires a more subtle form of shadowing. Mix small increments of black into a small puddle of Daisy Cream until you get a medium shade of warm gray. Use a small shader or flat brush to pick up paint, and wipe away much of it for drybrushing. Paint the shadows widest along the bottom of the head and neck, along the midsection between the front and rear hooves, and at the angle between the haunch and rear foot. Apply thinner shadows to the lower half of the rear portion of the haunch, along the top of the head, the tops of the haunches and the front legs.

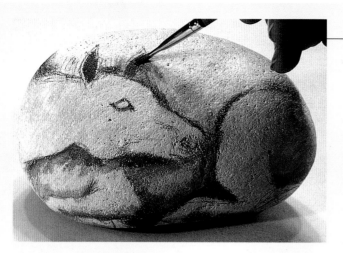

5| Deepen the Shadows

Add enough black to your gray mixture to darken it noticeably. Use a smaller flat or shader brush to pick up the paint, again wiping away any excess. Apply this darker gray in a narrow line to the area where the neck and round jawbone meet and also along the line from jaw to chin. Fill in the angle where the rear leg and haunch meet and the area along the base of the rock between the two hooves. Do the same to the backside of the rock. Finally, fill in the insides of the two ears with this dark gray.

6| Outline the Features

Switch to a liner brush and use black paint thinned slightly with water to define your zebra's features. Outline the eye, fill in the teardrop-shaped nostrils and go over the mouth line. Form an upright, striped mane by painting intermittent clusters between the ears and along the neck, but don't underline the base of these clusters. Go around the ears, head, haunch and legs. Outline the features on the backside as well. Once all the main elements are outlined, use more flowing lines to fill the tail. The tips of these tail strokes should reach nearly to the crook between the leg and haunch.

7| Draw on the Stripe Pattern

There are several zebra species, each with a slightly different look to its stripes. I chose the Grevy's Zebra and noted that even among members of this species there are some variations in the pattern. The stripes on the face and head are the most ornate and complex. If your rock shape dictates that your zebra faces the opposite direction from the one shown, try tracing over the pattern with waxed paper and a black permanent marker, then flip the paper over to see how the reversed pattern should look. Once adjusted to fit the size of your rock, you should be able to trace the stripes on if you prefer not to draw them freehand. Using a sharp pencil, draw two lines and fill in the area in between to draw each stripe. This way, you can vary the width of the stripes.

The stripes on the face start off very narrow at the nose and fan out from there to cover the head, getting both wider and more widely spaced as they go. One exception is the very narrow stripes running from nose to forehead; these tend to stay thin and closely spaced. Note that the stripes sometimes break or fork off at the tips. Such variations give the pattern its pleasing rhythm. A crooked line that goes from the front of the near ear to the jaw line transitions the pattern to more regular stripes along the neck. Take care not to match the stripes up with the clusters in the mane; offsetting them will look more natural.

The spine line begins where the top of the neck meets the end of the rock, then follows the top back edge of the rock across and down to the base of the tail. All the stripes for the body curve off from this central spine line.

In the midsection of the rock, the stripe pattern is again broken by a partial stripe. The stripes change direction at that point, curving in from the opposite direction to fill in the rest of the back.

On the haunches leave a narrow space along the top, making the first wide curved stripe just below it from front to back. Proceed to fill in the haunch with parallel lines that don't quite reach the front curve of the haunch. Give some of these stripes longer curves that sweep downward, and give others forked ends. Where the upper leg overlaps the haunch, break up the stripes so they don't line up evenly, suggesting a difference in the surfaces there. Curving the ends of the lines along the upper leg also suggests rounded contours. The stripes along the lower back leg should be more wedge-shaped and curved as if conforming to the shape of the leg. The tips should not reach the top of the leg.

Below the head, the stripes should seem to match up with the one above the head, then curve gracefully around the chest to join the stripes coming in from the other side. Along the very top of the front leg, just under the head, note that the stripes are short curves along the back edge that don't extend all the way across to the top.

It may take some time to figure out how the stripes fit together to make a pleasing whole, but the effort will pay off when you begin painting them.

8| Paint the Stripes

Select a flat brush small enough to maneuver in tight places. Use black paint to fill in the sketched-on stripe pattern. As you paint these stripes, turn your brush sideways often to add a bit of fringe along the edges rather than making them completely smooth. The wider the stripe, the more texture it should have. Begin with the spine line and body stripes, then move on to the back and front haunches. In the picture at left, I started with face stripes but decided it would be better to warm up on the bigger stripes.

Once the main stripes are in, switch to a liner brush to add the more delicate striping pattern to the face and the legs.

9| Paint the Muzzle

On an animal that is mainly black and white, the addition of even understated color has a big impact. Mix Patio Brick with a touch of black to get a deep, reddish brown and use a small round or flat brush with a soft bristle to paint the entire end of the muzzle and chin. Add more black to deepen the brown further, and use it to darken around and between the nostrils, leaving a narrow edge of the lighter brown around the nostrils, the mouth and lower lip.

10| Fill in the Eye

Use the tip of your liner brush and black paint to place a round pupil in the upper center of the eye shape. Mix in Patio Brick to create the same reddish brown first used on the muzzle and create a half-circle around the black pupil. Rinse your brush and make a narrow outline of straight Patio Brick along the very outside edge of the iris to give the eye more depth.

11| Tint the Back

Add a touch of Patio Brick to a small drop of Sunflower Yellow and mix with water until it is semi-transparent. With a medium flat brush, apply this tint in a wide swath between the black stripes on either side of the spine line. Pick up any excess along the edges with a paper towel or tissue. Also add a touch of this tint to the area of the haunch just above the tail but behind the leg crease.

12| Add Details to Face

All that remains are the small details that will bring this piece to life. Mix tiny amounts of Patio Brick and black to make a medium brown, then add an even tinier amount of white paint to lighten the mixture. Use it to underline the eye from corner to corner. I also used this lighter brown to encircle the nostrils, the edge of the upper lip and the curve of the lower lip, giving these features the additional definition they seemed to need.

13| Add White Details

Use the tip of your liner brush to add one or two tiny specks of white to the upper center of the eye and to add a fringe of ear fur sprouting from the inside edges of both ears.

14| Tint the Mane

Use your liner brush to add a trace of Sunflower Yellow to the white sections of the mane.

15| Darken the Roots

Add a touch of Patio Brick to the yellow and use this sparingly to darken just the roots.

16| Detail the Stripes

Use your liner brush and either black or white paint (perhaps both) to add tiny splinter strokes of texture to the wider stripes wherever they seem to be needed. Fringes of fur texture in white can help whittle down a black stripe that got too wide, or to reshape a stripe that doesn't quite seem to fit the pattern. In the same way, black fringes can widen stripes that are too thin or correct a curve.

17| Paint the Hooves

Mix a medium gray to fill in the two hooves showing at the very bottom of the piece.

18 | Add Final Touches

Look your zebra over carefully from every angle, searching for small flaws that can be easily corrected or minimized.

Allow the paint to dry, then spray the rock with clear acrylic sealer to heighten the colors and protect the paint.

Expand your zebra herd by making standing zebras. To do this, you will want to create an augmented neck to attach to your rock base. You can use pieces of gravel, glued together to build up the neck and head. This will give your zebra rock a graceful form that is strikingly realistic.

I used 521 Clear Glue to join pieces of gravel chosen for their shape and the way their facets fit together. Crumpled aluminum foil supports the gravel additions as they dry. Use a larger, more triangular-shaped piece for the head.

When dry, fill in the joints with wood filler and again cradle with foil, as the wood filler will soften the glue before both cure. The resulting bond will be surprisingly secure. You can also use wood filler to add more realistic contours to the head shape, building up the eye area and shaping the muzzle. I glued on bits of marble chips designed for fish aquariums to serve as ears.

For step-by-step instruction for creating an augmented neck, refer to the giraffe project on pages 90-91, steps 3 and 4.

Elephant Habitat

Despite their massive size, it is easy to see why these gentle giants are a favorite at any zoo. Watch them interact with other elephants, gently stroking one another with their trunks or leaning companionably together under the shade of a tree, and you will begin to appreciate how truly sociable and devoted they are to one another. At the zoo in Cincinnati, I was on hand as the keepers filled a wading pool for a baby elephant who paced impatiently until the gate was opened. It was such a delight to watch that little guy run and literally leap into the pool just as any three-year-old human might have done. The combination of size and intelligence makes elephants one of the most arresting and admirable members of the animal kingdom.

what you'll need

DecoArt Patio Paints in Wrought Iron Black · Cloud White · Pinecone Brown · Sunflower Yellow · large stiff-bristled flat brush · small and medium soft flat brushes · medium shader brushes · no. 0 or no. 1 liner brush · white-leaded pencil · template-making supplies, listed on page 10, optional · clear acrylic spray sealer

1 | Choose a Rock

The best rocks for elephants are rounded on top, with flat bottoms that allow them to stand. The sides should curve out, suggesting the bulk of this animal. One very rounded end might be perfect for an elephant in profile while a more blunt or angled end could suggest the turned head I used for this project. Once you've found your rock, scrub it and let it dry. My rock is a little over 5" (13cm) tall, 6" (15cm) long and 3" (8cm) wide. I've painted much larger ones and occasionally smaller ones.

2 | Basecoat Your Rock

Mix two parts white with one part black to get a medium shade of gray. Elephants come in colors that range from dark to light gray and sometimes even brown. Add one part Pinecone Brown (which I did for this project) or Sunflower Yellow to warm up the gray paint. Cover the rock quickly, using a large stiff-bristled brush.

3 | Sketch the Design

Copy the pattern freehand or make a template as described on page 9. Experiment with placement for the best fit on your rock.

Once the head is in place, the rest of this animal will be dictated by the contours of your individual rock. The front legs are like columns that taper out slightly at both ends. My rock's end is blunt, so I brought the front leg on the far side forward as though lifted in mid-step to fill in that corner of the rock. The other front leg is straight. The back legs are similar in shape, but seem shorter because the tummy line sags lower. Curving the upper portion of the leg line where it extends into the body gives the elephant's midsection a rounded look. Sketch in a second back leg just in front of the first one as though the rock is transparent. On the backside, place the straight front leg as if looking through the rock, then add the two back legs. You can change their position if needed since both sides can never be viewed at the same time. When painting your elephant, refer to these drawings again for placement of shading.

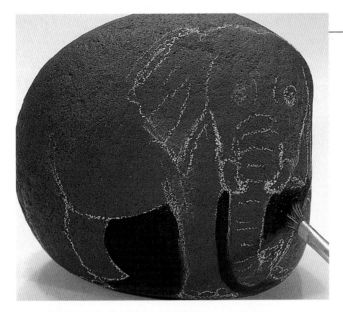

4| Paint Out the Voids

One challenge with animals that aren't curled up or crouching is that there may be large portions of rock that represent empty space. The best way to downplay such open spaces or voids is to fill them with black paint so that they seem to disappear. Use a small or medium-sized flat brush, switching to a liner for tight areas.

5| Paint Over the Guidelines

Use a liner brush and black paint to go over all the guidelines. It is vital that all elements be clearly defined, so paint the outlines bold rather than narrow or sketchy. Outline the eyes and surrounding wrinkles with finer lines. If remnants of your guidelines show, they can be removed later. Darken the opening at the tip of the trunk as well.

6| Create Shadows on Back of Rock

Mix black and Pinecone Brown in equal amounts to get a dark shade that is warmer than plain black. Use a medium-sized shader or flat brush, wiping away excess paint. Scrub on the paint, creating soft shadows where indicated on page 81. Start on the backside to get a feel for how these shadows should look. Shadowing the stomach in a U-shape heightens the illusion of roundness, but leave a narrow line of basecoat along the edge of the tummy to keep it distinct from the dark void below. Shadow the legs, extending some shadows around the legs in partial bands, especially at the midpoint where creases would naturally occur. Darken the very tops of the inside of the back legs on both sides of the rock so that these areas appear to be shadowed by the body. Paint a narrow shadow along the side of the tail just shy of the edge.

7 | Continue Shadows on Front

On the front add soft lines in the ears to suggest the look of folds. Shadow around and beneath the ears to help lift them away from the head. Make the head itself more distinct by encircling it with shadows that are widest along the lower half. On the face, use shadows to create sunken eye sockets surrounding the eyes. Move out from these sockets to create a second ring of soft shadows, leaving a lighter rim of basecoat in place to suggest bone structure. Bring a soft line of shadows down the center of the forehead, intersecting it with the outer shadow rims around each eye.

Shadow down the inside edge of the trunk, adding a few dark curving bands to suggest creases. Also shadow along the edge of the trunk tip where it curves up. The tusks extend from structures on either side of the trunk and these, too, should be shadowed as shown to suggest dimension.

Shade the sides of the legs, again including more curved bands for creases. Darken along the bottom of the stomach, leaving a narrow strip of lighter basecoat in place along the edge to define it. Note how the shadow along the curve of the stomach reaches up to blend with the shadows around the head and front leg.

8 | Create Heavy Highlights

Mix a small amount of black into white paint to get a shade of gray clearly lighter than the original basecoat. Add a touch of Pinecone Brown to warm the color slightly. Use the same brush used for shadowing, again wiping away excess paint to get a soft, dry-brush effect. Highlight all areas opposite those you just shadowed. Paint them heaviest along the tops of features including the shoulder and along either side of the center spine, the top curve of the head and the tops of the ears. Also apply the highlight to a leg if it's lifted as on my elephant. Lessen the highlights as you work down the elephant.

On the face, play up the ring of basecoat around the eyes by highlighting it, then feather paint out into the cheek areas. Add curves of highlighting to the trunk between the shadowed creases. Give just a touch of highlighting to the tusk socket on the right side. On the ears, place highlights next to shadows to emphasize the look of folds. Highlight along the sides of each front leg as well as along the trunk opposite the shadowed side. Accentuate the shadowy creases along the top of the trunk by adding lighter bands between them. Also highlight along the other side of the tail.

When you highlight the back legs, extend a line of lighter paint along the upper thigh to emphasize the curve of the

stomach. Allow highlights to grow fainter and stop altogether about one-third of the way down. Highlights and shadows work together with the neutral basecoat and the shape of the rock itself to create a magical transformation!

9| Add Finer Highlights

Switch to a liner brush and add a bit more white to your highlighting shade to brighten it. Loosen the paint slightly by adding small increments of water. Use the tip of the brush to go around the outside edges of the ears, face and sockets of the tusks. Completely outline around the trunk, including the opening at the tip. Go around both sides of all the legs. Reinforce the highlighting along the curve of the stomach. Add narrow horizontal lines of this lighter highlighting down the center of the trunk and at the knees of all four legs. On the near front leg, curve the lines into loose circles at the knee. Move to the eyes and highlight between the darker bags and wrinkles. Add small crescent-shaped lids just above and below the eyes as well as crow's feet to the outer corners to give them more character.

Once these main features have been emphasized, begin adding texture to the skin, creating a random grid of fine lines and wrinkles that crisscross in thin curves as shown on page 81. Making sets of two or three strokes in a variety of directions will help keep them random-looking.

Add a row of short lines along the highlighted edge of the tail, then stroke in a cluster to form a tassel at the tip.

10| Layer on More Fine Lines

Elephants are known for their baggy, wrinkled skin. Play up this distinctive trait by creating a layer of fine, dark lines. Use black, softened slightly by the addition of half as much Pinecone Brown and again loosen the consistency so paint will flow easily from the tip of your liner brush. Start by adding lines between the fine lines of highlighting down the center of the trunk. Outline around the upper and lower eyelids. Add dark lines between the crow's feet and along the brow ridge, flaring the lines out almost like lashes. Make a set of lines that follow the curve of the forehead and more that arch out from the base of the ears.

11| Add Lines to Body

On the body, intersperse these dark lines among the lighter ones. Use them to play up the vaguely circular pattern at the knees. On the flank and the tummy, use dark lines to reinforce the lighter crisscrosses below them and also to add texture to areas that have few or no wrinkles.

12| Paint the Eyes

Use Pinecone Brown and your liner brush to fill in the eyes within their dark outlines. There is often a temptation to enlarge the eyes and give them more emphasis, but oversized eyes will give this animal a cartoonish look or make it appear to be a much younger elephant. If needed, use black to smooth out the eye edges or reestablish the outlines.

13| Paint the Tusks and Toes

Soften white paint with a touch of Pinecone Brown to make an ivory color. Fill in the tusks and give each foot three neat half-round toes.

14| Finish the Eyes

Use black and the tip of your liner brush to add a tiny black pupil to the upper center of each eye. When dry, make an even smaller dot of white at the upper edge of the pupil to give the elephant's eyes a lifelike gleam.

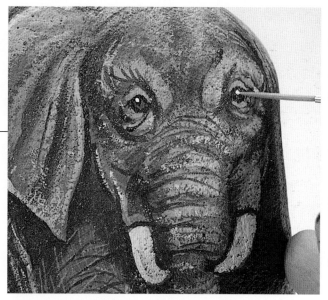

15| Add Grass

Minimize the starkness of the empty black spaces around the legs by mixing a touch of Sunflower Yellow into a small amount of white paint to get a pale golden yellow. Use your liner brush to stroke in long blades of grass from the base of the rock upward as shown. Make some of the stems slant sideways as though flattened by those big feet.

An elephant calf could also be placed among the legs to fill up this blank space.

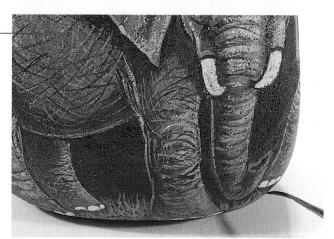

16 | Add Finishing Touches

Now look your elephant over from every angle to make sure you have sufficient details. I decided that the dark area below the head on the right side looked unfinished, so I mixed up a little gray paint and added a couple curved strokes in the center to suggest wrinkled skin showing at the chest.

Allow the paint to dry, then spray the rock with a light coat of clear acrylic sealer to heighten your colors and protect the paint. Matte or satin is best on very smooth rocks where gloss sealers may create distracting gleams.

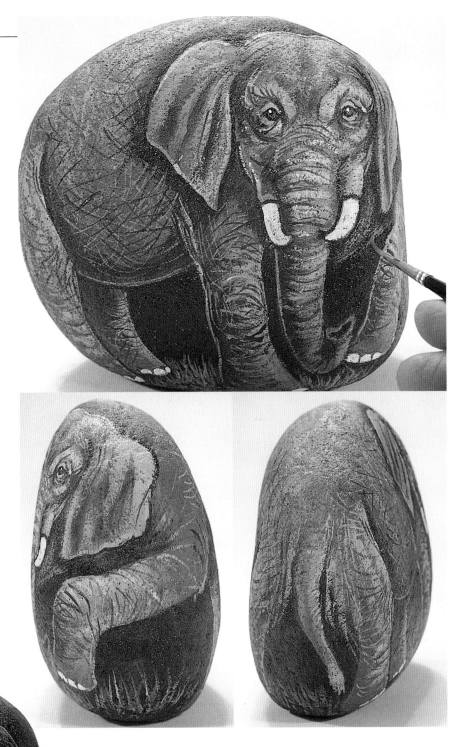

This rock's unusual shape inspired me to try painting from a photo of a baby elephant I came across. I added the ball to fill out the rock shape.

Start collecting elephant photos and you are likely to see many other ways you can fit these majestic animals onto rocks.

More zoo animals to paint

Painting a walrus, with its tusks and wrinkled skin, is very similar to painting the elephant.

Walrus

When painting a walrus, look for a humped rock like those used for elephants. Leave the natural rock unpainted to serve as the base. Mix up a pale gray paint and add Geranium Red to get the pinkish color common to sunbathing walruses. The wrinkled skin texture is identical to the elephant's.

Giraffe Savanna

Would a trip to the zoo be complete without seeing giraffes? Yet fitting a giraffe's elongated neck and stilt-like legs onto a rock is a real challenge. You might get lucky and happen upon an extremely unusual rock shape. If not, there is another solution. It requires a bit of ingenuity and patience, but the reward is a unique and graceful creation that will have admirers asking, "How'd you do that?"

what you'll need

DecoArt Patio Paints in Wrought Iron Black · Daisy Cream · Cloud White · Patio Brick · Pinecone Brown · Sunflower Yellow · multi-purpose cement · wood filler (1.25 oz. tube preferred) · several sheets of aluminum foil · pencil · large stiff-bristled flat brush · small and medium soft flat and round brushes · no. 0 or no. 1 liner brush · template-making supplies, listed on page 10, optional · clear acrylic spray sealer

1| Choose a Rock

Start by selecting a narrow, upright rock with a flat base. A top that is slightly sloped rather than symmetrically rounded is a plus. Make sure the rock is well scrubbed and thoroughly dry. Despite the differences between them, all of these rocks are good candidates to transform into giraffes. The rock I chose is on the left; it's 7" (18cm) tall at the highest end, 4" (10cm) across and 2" (5cm) wide. The top is sloped, which will add to the realistic look.

2| Steady the Base

While good, my rock is not perfect because the base is uneven. I added two small bits of gravel, gluing them in place where the feet would be.

3| Attach Neck Base

Collect an assortment of gravel pieces or small pebbles that can be combined to form a long tapering neck. Like a puzzle, it may take some mixing and matching to find the best combination. Take your base rock along to fit the first piece to the surface it will be glued to. A perfect fit is not required, but construction will be easier if the shapes match up at least somewhat.

Turn the individual pieces around and try fitting together different sides to form a tapering column. Choose a more elongated piece to serve as the head. For my 7" (17cm) tall rock, the neck and head additions totaled 4" (10cm). Once you find a combination that works, keep the pieces in proper order by numbering them and by drawing a line along one side to indicate how they match up.

Use multi-purpose cement to glue the first piece of gravel to the body of the giraffe rock. Press and hold a few minutes until it begins to set, or lay the larger rock on its side and use crumpled aluminum foil to support the gravel until the glue dries. Allow at least five hours for a secure set.

4| Assemble the Neck

Meanwhile, glue the remaining pieces of gravel together to form the neck, cradling them in a piece of crumpled foil. When the glue is thoroughly dry, attach this neck section to the base, laying the rock on its side and using crumpled foil to support both sides as they dry. The edges of gravel may be uneven, but you can cover them with wood filler later to smooth them out.

5| Attach the Head

Stand the rock up and turn it to find the best match of surfaces for bonding the head-shaped gravel piece to the neck. The head can be set on facing straight ahead, tipped up or down or even turned slightly. The surfaces of the two rocks you are joining will likely dictate the direction of the head. If the angle looks unnatural, add a thin sliver or wedge of rock to the neck to change the surface and try again once it dries.

The resulting neck may curve or twist in a way that can be graceful or even whimsical. Due to the nature of the gravel pieces and the way they fit together, your giraffe will have its own unique look. Once it is dry, stand your piece up and check it out from various directions. If you aren't happy with the way the construction turned out, you can snap it apart at any point, exchange one of the pieces or refit a joint. Just make sure you allow the repair to set thoroughly before going on.

6| Fill in the Joints

Because the wood filler will soften the cement, use just enough filler to fill the gaps, lessening the risk of over-softening the glue. Squeeze the wood filler out into the crevices at the joints and smooth it with a wet fingertip to keep it from sticking to your skin.

To ensure that the pieces stay together, use the foil to cradle the neck and head while this first application of wood filler dries, which should not take more than an hour or two.

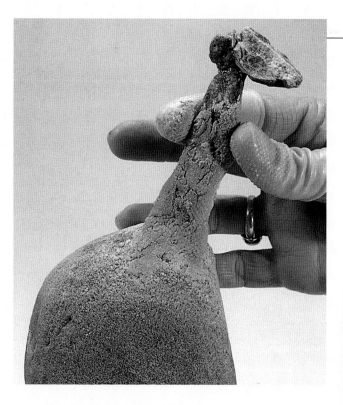

7| Cover Over the Additions

Once the filler is dry, cover the entire construction with sufficient filler to shape the neck into a smooth column. Use the wood filler to modify or enhance the head by adding a muzzle and indented nostrils along with rounded protuberances where the eyes will be. Along the back of the neck you can pinch up a small ridge for the giraffe's short mane. Remember that keeping fingers wet prevents the wood filler from sticking. You may also use rubber gloves or little fingertip protectors. Lay the rock down and cradle the newly covered neck in aluminum foil while it dries. If at any point your construction comes apart, glue it back together and again wait overnight to add filler.

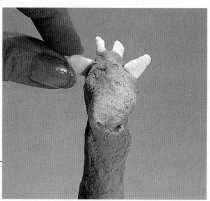

8| Add Ears and Horns

At the top back of the head, build up a heavy ridge and insert two small, cylindrical rock slivers to form horns. Next select a pair of matching flat oval pieces for the ears. White marble chips used to cover the bottoms of fish aquariums make excellent ears and horns. They attach more securely if the ends are flat, and these chips are easily clipped with a pair of sturdy scissors. Use a tiny drop of glue on either side of the top of the head, pressing and holding the ears in place for several minutes until they stay. Once the glue dries, use wood filler to cover the joints at the base. The tip of a paintbrush or a toothpick makes a good tool for smoothing and shaping the filler as it dries.

9| Sketch on the Features

Use a pencil to sketch on the legs and the curved, slanting line of the tummy. Generally the legs will be about the same length as the neck and head, but yours will depend on your rock. It is better to have overly long legs than too bulky a body.

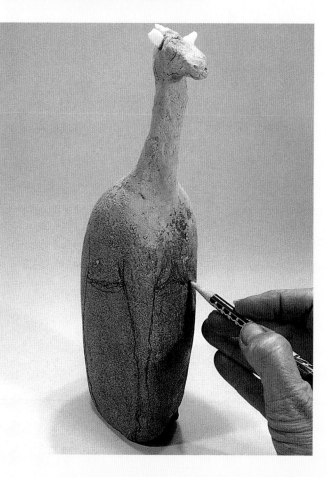

The back legs have distinctive crooks while the front legs have rounded, knobby knees. You can sketch on the legs freehand or create templates from the pattern (as described on page 9) to trace around. Since every rock is a little different, try to fit your legs to the angles of your rock as much as possible. Slant the stomach line down from front to back. At the rear end draw a narrow, tapering tail that hangs nearly to the base of the rock.

When you're placing the spots, refer to these drawings again for guidance.

10| Paint the Basecoat

Use black paint and a large stiff-bristled flat brush to fill in the spaces around and between all the legs and around the tail in back. Switch to Daisy Cream to fill in the giraffe. You may need a smaller brush to paint the tail.

For subtle contrast, use white paint to lighten the lower third of the body all the way around, as well as along the inside curves of the back legs down to the crooks. Add white to the area along the lower jaw and down the front of the neck halfway down. Extend the white at the chest down along the sides of the legs to the knees.

11| Add Shadows

Start with a small drop of Daisy Cream and add a touch of black, just enough to get a medium shade of gray. Choose a small, worn brush to pick up this paint, wiping away much of it so that the remainder must be scrubbed on. Apply this gray in a slight curve just above the tummy so that a very narrow line of light paint remains uncovered along the edge. Bring both ends of these shadows up to where the haunch and upper front legs join the body. These U-shaped shadows partially overlap but should not cover all the white basecoating.

12| Choose a Markings Pattern

There are several distinctive species of giraffe, each with its own pattern of markings. Some have irregular patches; others have lighter colors in the centers of their markings, while still others have markings with very tidy edges and even spaces. I prefer the look of a more ornate pattern, in the center, but you may choose a plainer one if you wish.

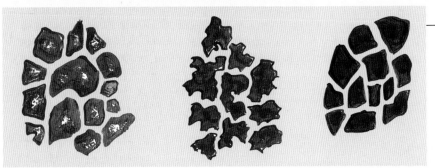

13| Sketch on the Markings

Use a sharpened pencil to sketch on guidelines, starting with the smaller, more sparse markings around the head. As you work your way down the neck and over the chest and back, increase the size of the patches. Let the pattern evolve so that, while the markings are very diverse, the spaces surrounding them remain the same width, creating a pleasing sense of consistency. As you reach the legs, the patterns should grow smaller and simpler in shape until they stop about halfway down. Don't make markings along the tummy. One exception to the overall randomness of the pattern is the spine, where the markings should form a sort of blocky line of squared-off shapes from the bottom of the neck to the top of the tail. Guidelines for these markings need not be perfect. It is likely you will make changes as you paint them in.

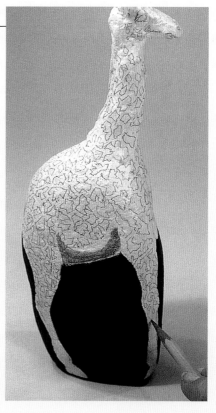

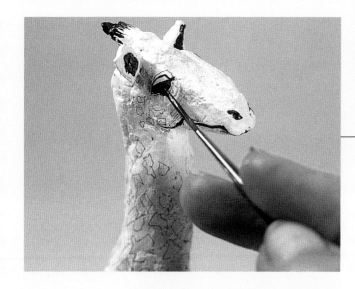

14| Paint Facial Features

Begin with a small puddle of Patio Brick, adding in enough black to get a very deep brown that is nearly black. Use a damp liner brush to outline and then fill in the centers of both ears, and to darken the tips of the horns. Paint in the nostrils and give the giraffe a mouth line on both sides as shown on the pattern. Use the tip of the brush to carefully paint a heavy-lidded eye on each side just below the ears, and fill in the entire eye circle.

15| Paint the Mane

Switch to a slightly larger flat brush and use this same dark brown to paint the mane down the center of the backside of the neck. Darken in the flowing fur at the tip of the tail.

16| Outline the Markings

Add more Patio Brick to your mixture to get a color that is still dark but more reddish brown. Then add a bit of water to help the paint flow smoothly off the tip of your liner brush. Outline the markings, adding more jags if you like.

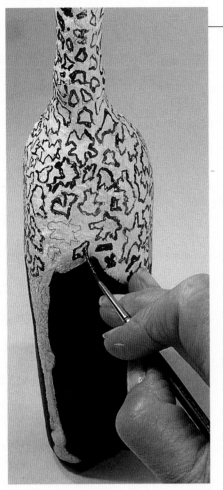

17| Fill in the Markings

Once they are all outlined, lighten the mix with more Patio Brick, and use a small flat or round brush to fill in the markings. Don't go all the way to the edges of the chest or hind end. Before moving to the next step, switch to a liner brush and use straight Patio Brick paint to add a U shape to each eye, leaving a dark center and edges.

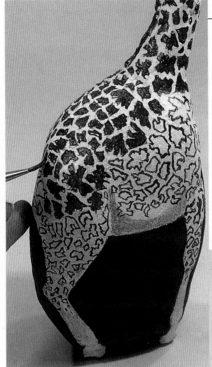

18| Tint the Shoulders and Back

Mix equal parts Pinecone Brown and Patio Brick and add enough water to make the mixture soupy. Use a soft brush to pick up this watery pigment, and wipe off enough to prevent dripping. Apply to the rock with scrubbing motions, starting about two-thirds of the way down the neck and fanning outward down the back and sides. Avoid tinting the tummy area. Extend the tint down the centers of the front and back legs, stopping halfway down the lower portions of the legs. Leave the edges light.

This pale warm tint pulls the marking pattern together and contrasts pleasingly with the areas not tinted. Scrubbing on the wash keeps it soft looking and also helps remove pencil marks that weren't covered up.

19| Tint the Forehead and Face

Use the same color on the head from the base of the horns down to the muzzle, leaving the eyes and the sides of the face plain. Add tint to the area just below the ears on either side of the head, and run a narrow line of tint down the neck on either side of the mane.

20| Paint the Feet

Add a small amount of black to white paint to get a deep gray and use a small brush to fill in the hooves all the way around. The rear hooves are simple curved tops with wider curved bottoms, while the front hooves have a slight dip in the center of the upper line as shown.

21| Add White Detail

With the liner brush, give each eye a tiny dot of white in the center. Add a fringe of tiny white fur lines to the inside edge of each ear.

22| Add Dark Detail

Mix a touch of Patio Brick with black and apply with a dry brush to softly darken the center of the forehead, narrowing to two parallel lines down the face, then widening again to darken the center of the muzzle.

23| Paint the Void

Because the legs are so long, the spaces between a giraffe's legs are quite large. You can leave them starkly black, or soften their impact by adding details. To do so, mix equal parts of Sunflower Yellow and Daisy Cream, with just 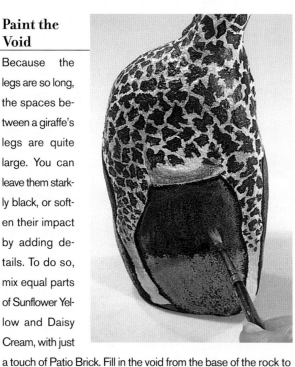 a touch of Patio Brick. Fill in the void from the base of the rock to a horizontal line just below the knees. Turn the rock, extending this horizon to all the sides, but leave dark margins of basecoat in place surrounding the legs and the tail. Add enough water to the mixture to create a filmy wash and use this to fill in and soften the remaining upper portions of the voids, again leaving dark margins around the edges of the legs and below the tummy.

24| Add Grass

Switch to a liner brush and mix Sunflower Yellow and Daisy Cream to stroke in some tall grass stems. Stroke upward from the base to just past the horizon lines on all the sides. Allow the grass to have a random look, with some strokes longer or more angled and others short and straight. Allow the paint to dry, and then spray the rock with clear acrylic sealer to heighten the colors and protect the paint.

25| See How Strong it Is

Like porcelain, dropping the rock or knocking the piece over can damage the neck, but when the additions have been cemented carefully and well covered with wood filler, the resulting piece is both attractive and surprisingly sturdy. I can lift up my augmented rock by the addition and even sling it about without hurting it.

Each of these giraffes sports a different pattern of markings. Variations in both the basic rock shape and the way the addition comes together ensures that every giraffe you create will be unique! If you can't find a suitable rock for a standing giraffe, try making a baby with its legs curled beneath its body like the one shown on page 88.

Use your imagination to think of other ways to use augmentation to enhance your rock animals. Here I've created tusks and a trunk for a truly dimensional elephant!

Welcome to the
Petting Zoo

Whether you have a child in tow or are a child-at-heart yourself, the petting zoo portion of any zoo is a special place and not to be missed. Where else can you interact one-on-one with a variety of tame and gentle creatures? Some petting zoos feature mainly young farm animals, now increasingly exotic to our more urbanized population. Other petting areas offer animals ranging from rabbits and mice to guinea pigs and hedgehogs. Here is a chance to feel the texture of a lamb's woolly coat, be tickled by the scratchy toenails of a small rodent or stroke a newly hatched chick. My children recall being surrounded by a flock of inquisitive kid goats that nibbled at their shoelaces and sampled strands of their hair. At another petting zoo we cuddled a litter of young piglets as they tumbled about at our feet. Such hands-on encounters have helped us realize how wonderful and exciting animal life is in all its varied forms.

Chicken Coop

Newly hatched chicks, fuzzy but still egg-shaped, are a fun and easy subject to paint.

They make an adorable addition to an Easter display, too. Allow the shape of the rock

to guide you in the placement of the chick's head. Look for slight bulges or contours

that suggest where the head might be. This project features a "heads up" pose, but

chicks also look cute with their heads lowered as if pecking at a tasty morsel.

what you'll need

DecoArt Patio Paints in Tiger Lily Orange · Wrought Iron
Black · Patio Brick · Geranium Red · Sunflower Yellow ·
Sunshine Yellow · Cloud White · pencil · paint primer,
optional · medium stiff-bristled brush, optional · small and
medium soft flat and round brushes · no. 0 or no. 1 liner brush ·
template-making supplies, listed on page 10, optional · clear
acrylic spray sealer

1| Select a Rock

Find a small, smooth oval rock, scrub it well and let it dry. The rock doesn't have to be perfectly oval. Mine has one more pointed end. But it should sit solidly. A line of wood filler at the base can help stabilize a rock that doesn't have a flat bottom. If the rocks in your area are extremely hard and smooth, a coat of primer, such as Kilz, provides a sturdy foundation and also provides a light base for dark rocks.

2| Paint the Basecoat Color

Paint the rock with Tiger Lily Orange. If your rock is dark, you may need to apply two coats, or start with a coat of Sunshine Yellow then cover it with Tiger Lily Orange to get a bright color. Use a stiff-bristled or scruffy flat brush to cover the entire visible area of the rock.

3| Sketch the Design

The layout for this rock could hardly be easier, but you can create a template from the patterns as described on page 9. Use a sharp pencil to give the chick a large oval head that takes up approximately half of the frontal rock area. The head can be placed high as mine is or lower on the rock's front as if the chick is about to peck at something on the ground. On both sides sketch in smaller and narrower ovals for the wings, bringing them to a point toward the tail while leaving the other end open. Just above the base of the rock sketch in a curving line that defines the bottom of the chick while leaving room below to fit the feet. This line can be higher at the head end then swoop down almost to the base below the tail. The legs angle in from a point below the back tips of the wings. Each narrow leg has one back toe and three curving front toes. Add small, widely spaced eyes and a triangular beak to complete the layout.

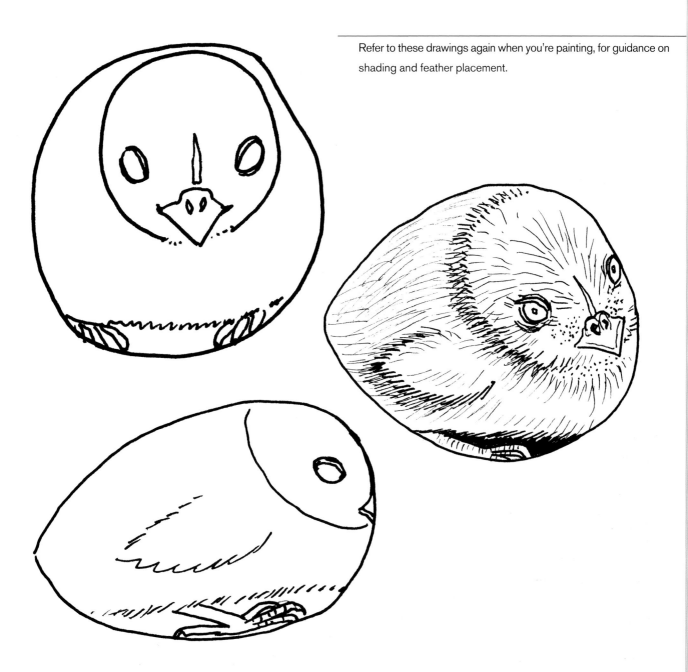

Refer to these drawings again when you're painting, for guidance on shading and feather placement.

4| Paint the Void

Use black paint to fill in the void below the bottom of the chick. Use a small or medium round or flat brush but switch to a liner to paint around the legs and feet.

5 | Establish Contours

Mix Patio Brick with just enough black paint to get a deep reddish brown shade. Use a worn flat brush to pick up the paint, wiping away most of it so that the remainder must be scrubbed on. Scrub the paint all around the head, stroking outward. Do the same for the wings along the bottom edge and just barely around the tip. Use this same color and a liner brush to outline the chick's eyes and beak.

6 | Fill in the Feet and Beak

Start with a small drop of Sunflower Yellow and add tiny increments of Geranium Red until you get a very soft, warm pink. Use this and a small brush to fill in the beak. Switch to a liner brush to fill in the leg and the long, tapering toes. Though subtle, the legs, feet and beak are a clearly different shade than the body.

7 | Layer Feathers on the Head

Start with a small puddle of Sunshine Yellow paint and add just enough water so the paint flows off the tip of your liner brush without being so watery it is runny or transparent. Begin with the outside edges of the head, stroking outward from within the oval to create a clearly defined border of very short, dense splinter lines. Move inward half a stroke and create a second layer that partially overlaps the first, but is not quite as short or dense. Continue working inward until you near the base of the beak, leaving a bit of the orange basecoat showing there. Also leave edges of orange basecoat uncovered around the outsides of the eyes. A narrow line of orange should remain visible right above the beak as well. Refer to the drawings on page 105 for guidance.

8| Add Feathers to Body

Once the head is done, work on the rest of the chick. Leave a narrow gap between the tips of feather spikes surrounding the head and the ones that will cover the body, allowing the shading to help separate and define the two areas. Paint the strokes slightly denser around elements needing to be defined, like the wings. Always work away from the head, with each stroke directed toward the tail as you add layer upon layer until the entire chick is covered.

9| Detail the Face

Use plain black paint on a liner brush to fill in the small oval eye shapes. Underline the V shape of the beak and give it two small nostrils like teardrops. Mix white and Sunshine Yellow to create a pale yellow. Use it to outline the eyes and to outline the inside edge of the beak and the top curves of the nostrils.

10| Paint Pale Yellow Feathers

Still using very pale yellow and your liner brush, add another layer of short spikes around the head, then work into the center of the head as before with this lighter shade. On the body, concentrate the pale spikes in the center of the breast, the tops of the wings, and less densely along the bottom wing edge. Sprinkle them more randomly down the backside.

11 | Detail the Legs and Feet

Still using pale yellow and the tip of a liner brush, add a row of tiny, curving lines to the top edge of each leg and even tinier lines to the tops of the toes. These delicate lines give the legs the look of scaly texture. Add a small crescent-shaped nail at the tip of each toe.

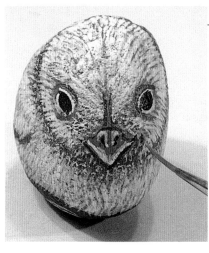

12 | Finish the Face

With Patio Brick and the liner, outline the eyes and paint parallel lines above the beak. Use a tiny bit of Patio Brick on the tip of your liner to create small speckles between the beak and the eyes and below the beak, to indicate the stubbly feathers growing there.

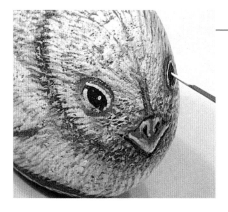

13 | Finish the Eyes

Add a speck of white paint in each eye to make it seem like the chick is looking back at you.

14 | Brighten the Feathers

Use Sunshine Yellow on your liner brush to add more speckles around the beak and along the lower half of the neck. Sprinkle yellow spikes among the pale ones in the center of the head and throughout the body to rev up the color a bit.

Allow the paint to dry, then spray the rock with clear acrylic sealer to heighten the colors and protect the paint.

smooth the surface by placing a small square of plastic over it and rubbing. Create jagged edges all the way around using the tip of a knife to cut and remove filler in a random way. Paint the eggshell white when it has dried.

For the mother hen, I found a perfect, plump oval rock and added just enough wood filler to build up the comb atop the hen's head. I glued a chunky rock to the back of the rock, covered the joints with wood filler and angled out the sides to form a perky set of tail feathers.

Cover the rock with dark brown made by mixing Patio Brick and black paint. Use black to surround and set off the head and create the curve of the neck, then switch to a smaller brush and use black to layer on V-shaped feathers down the neck and chest and to create a more scalloped looking pattern of feathers along the back and sides.

Mix Sunflower Yellow and white and use this pale gold to highlight and detail the feather pattern and to surround the eye on the head and highlight the edges of the beak. Paint the comb and wattles Geranium Red with a bit of Sunflower Yellow added. Use a liner brush and Patio Brick to add more details and shadings to the feathers.

For the chick in the shell, I used wood filler to create the eggshell hat. Squeeze out a marble-sized dollop of filler on top of the painted chick and allow it to sit for about a minute to lose its initial stickiness. Use a wet finger or damp sponge to flatten the filler over the top of the rock, and then

More zoo animals to paint

Give another feathered friend a try—this little duckling is painted much like the chick.

Duckling

Domestic ducklings are yellow, just like chicks, but wild varieties, such as this baby mallard, have more dramatic markings. Use more white in the layers of downy feathers to make a paler gold color. Then mix black and Patio Brick to make a deep brown for the markings.

Piglet Pen

Like lambs, young pigs are nearly irresistible. Small, sleek and squirming piglets are also inquisitive, bright and fun to watch. Their moist snouts will prod and poke anyone and anything within reach. Hold one too tight and its squeal will signal loudly that it wants to be released. Many people collect pig art and would welcome the addition of a hand-painted rock piglet.

what you'll need

DecoArt Patio Paints in Daisy Cream · Geranium Red · Patio Brick · Wrought Iron Black · Cloud White · Sunflower Yellow · medium or large stiff-bristled flat brush· small flat and small round soft brushes · no. 0 or no. 1 liner · pencil · template-making supplies, listed on page 10, optional · clear acrylic spray sealer

1| Select a Rock

The main consideration when selecting a piglet rock is roly-poly proportions and enough height to fit the ears either standing up or with folded-over tips. A flat base and plump oval shape make this little rock a good choice.

2| Paint the Basecoat

A deep, dusky pink basecoat is needed to help set off the lighter fur details. Mix equal parts Geranium Red and Daisy Cream. Use a medium or large stiff-bristled flat brush to cover the entire visible surface of the rock.

3| Sketch the Design

Once the paint has dried, you can create a template from the pattern provided, as described on page 9, or simply sketch the features with a pencil. Draw the head as a rounded shape, with the snout lines angling out as if to form a triangle. Rather than coming to a point, shorten the snout and give it a semi-circular flat end. Add a rounded angle on the head for the unseen eye and draw the ears. Draw the haunches slightly smaller than the head, and tuck the legs and hooves along the bottom edge.

Refer to these drawings again when you're painting for guidance on placement of shading and on fur direction.

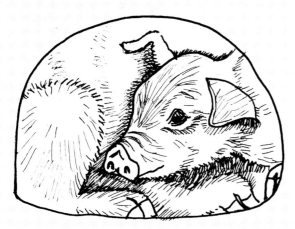

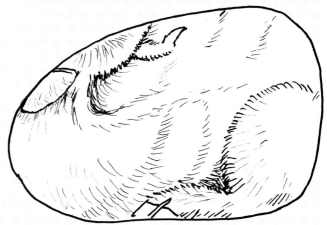

4| Outline the Features

Mix a small amount of Patio Brick into your basecoat color then add increments of black until you have a deep brown color with reddish undertones. Use this color on a damp liner brush to go over all the pencil lines that define your piglet's features. The outlines should not be overly thick, but make them solid rather than sketchy. Don't forget the little curly tail!

5| Add an Undercoat of Dark Fur Lines

Loosen the same paint color slightly with a drop of water and apply fur lines with the tip of your liner brush. Study the lines on page 112 for help with direction. Angle your strokes along the top of the snout, then fan them up and out over the forehead between the eye and the bump where the second eye is unseen. Make a heavier row of strokes above the eye, and another row along the bottom of the eye as shown. Along the bottom of the jaw extend a row of strokes running parallel with the mouth line into the cheek area, and a second cluster of lines that shadows the curve of the head between the back of the jaw and the edge of the lower ear. Add a crescent of dark fur lines to the lower inside curve of the haunches on both sides of the rock.

6| Create Shadowy Contours

Switch to a small flat brush and pick up the same dark color used for outlines and fur, but wipe excess pigment from your brush so that the remaining paint must be scrubbed on vigorously for a soft look without sharp edges. Use this dry-brush method to create deep shadows below the head and at the crook of the back legs on both sides of the rock. Go along the outside edges of the head and haunches with a wide swath of dark shadow. Apply a heavy shadow between the forehead and the crook of the upper ear, and a smaller shadow below the lower ear. Don't shadow the tops of either ear. Along the top of the head extend the shadowing slightly to suggest the curve of the spine. Add two curved bands of shadow to the midsection of the pig on both sides. Also darken the spaces below the legs at the bottom edge of the rock.

7| Layer on Light Pink Fur Lines

Mix up a small batch of the basecoat color using equal parts of Geranium Red and Daisy Cream, then add enough white to get a clearly lighter shade. Use a dampened liner brush to apply this light pink color in a solid mat of overlapping strokes. Check the fur directional guide on page 112 for help in angling these strokes properly as you work away from the nose, down the back and toward the rear end of the rock. On the haunch allow a few strokes to angle upward along the top without obscuring the underlying out-

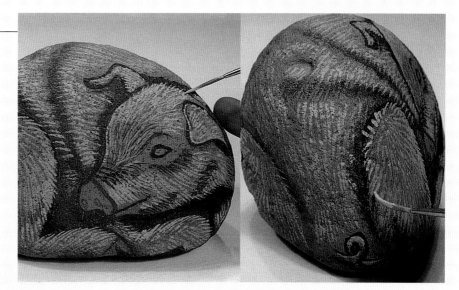

lines. From there move around the curve of the haunch with short, splinter-type strokes. Once you are finished with this step, your entire piglet should be covered with a layer of pink fur excepting the dark shadows where the tips of your fur strokes encroach only slightly. Define the lower ear shape by creating a light outline around its tip right next to the dark outline.

8| Paint Reddish Details

Mix equal parts Sunflower Yellow and Geranium Red to get a warm, reddish orange. Use a liner or other small brush to fill in the cloven hooves on all of the feet. Straddle a few strokes across the bridge of the nose, and surround the eye with this warm color as well. Fill in the flat end of the snout, too. If you opted to give your piglet upright ears, use this color inside them.

9| Add Highlights

Add white to to the mix from step 8 to make a clearly lighter shade and use it to highlight the top edges of the hooves and the top curve of the snout's flat end.

10 | Paint Black Details

With black paint on the liner, add two inverted U-shaped nostrils to the snout, then fill in the eye shape with solid black. Also extend the split between each hoof up into the foot.

11 | Paint White Details

The addition of a layer of white fur lines will give your piglet its characteristic silvery appearance. White fur also increases the degree of contrast between dark and light areas. Add just enough water to your white paint to loosen it so that it will flow easily off the tip of your liner brush. Go around the edges of your features with a tight row of white splinter strokes, placing them over and around the pink ones you painted earlier. Angle them along the edges of the folded legs and right along the edges of the dark curved lines around the piglet's midsection. When working along the top of the head you may find it helpful to turn the rock upside down. Fan these white fur strokes out over the forehead above the dark lines between the eyes. Add rows of tiny strokes to the chin and along the bottom of the head. Surround the eye with light strokes that remain just outside the darker strokes made there earlier. Add three or four strokes that curve along the top of the bridge of the snout. Don't forget to add white fur layers to the back and ends of the rock.

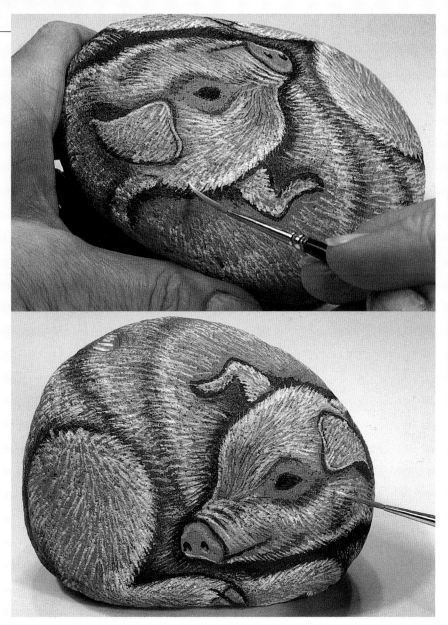

12| Add Golden Details

Before changing colors, add a very narrow half-circle of white to the bottom of the eye, leaving a thin margin of black around the outside edge.

Mix Sunflower Yellow and white paint together to get a pale gold. Sprinkle fur lines of this soft color in amongst the others, mainly down the center of the face, the center of the haunches and lightly through the dark bands of shadowing in the midsection to soften and integrate them. These warm golden fur lines and highlights create a bridge between darker and lighter colors that helps create a soft blending effect. Add pale gold fur lines to the centers of the legs as well, and sprinkle a few in the center of the shadowed area above the crook of the back leg. Do the same in the shadowed area between the two front legs, leaving the outer edges dark. Add an eyelid above the eye and a bit of highlighting below the eye.

13| Paint Reddish Brown Details

Mix Patio Brick with just enough black to darken it to a deep reddish brown and use this to add a small inverted V in the upper half of the flattened snout. Underline around the bottoms of the nostrils, coming up slightly between them to create a short, rounded W. Use this color to add a crease around the upper eyelid and to darken and extend the half-circle of shadowing below the eye. Add a light sprinkling of reddish brown fur to the forehead. Also use it to soften the edges of shadowing around the head and below the tips of the ears. Look for other areas that would benefit from a bit of this detail, but avoid the outside edges of white fur where you want to maintain strong contrast. Don't neglect the backside.

14| Add Finishing Touches

Ordinarily I add a speck of white to my subject's eyes, but piglets have long eyelashes that keep the sparkle from showing. Instead, use pale gold (see step 12) to create a few slanting lash lines along the top of the eye, leaving an edge of the black eye color in place between them. Look your piglet over to make sure all areas are sufficiently detailed.

Allow the paint to dry, then spray the rock with clear acrylic sealer to heighten the colors and protect the paint.

Piglets can be painted in a variety of poses. The rock I painted could also have been done as a head-on view with ears up as the one in the foreground was.

My favorite piglets are the silvery pink ones, but you may prefer to paint speckled or spotted versions. To paint this pig, cover the rock with pink fur. When dry, tint the entire rock with a watery mix of Sunflower Yellow and Patio Brick. Add random black patches, using the tip of a liner to give them fringed edges. Do the same with the white patches.

More zoo animals to paint

Another favorite petting zoo animal is the hedgehog. I made my hedgehog rock "reversible" by painting a different view on each side!

Hedgehog

To paint your hedgehog, mark off the entire white area and paint the remaining area very dark brown using black mixed with a small amount of Patio Brick. Paint the spines with the tip of a liner brush and Patio Brick. When dry, add white tips to all the spines. Paint the white area gray first, and then build up the white fur in layers, allowing some fine fur to overlap into the dark areas. Paint the muzzle with Geranium Red and white plus a touch of black. The paws are pinker, so don't add black to the mix for them, and use more red to outline the fingers. Paint the ears gray with lighter gray edges.

Lamb's Run

From their soft, stuttering *baaas* to the sweet innocence of their wide-set eyes, lambs are incredibly appealing animals. It's impossible to imagine not reaching out to rub that velvet muzzle or pat that fleecy coat. When they are in the mood to frolic, lambs will kick up their heels and leap about in a way that seems to characterize the term "youthful exuberance." Lamb and lion rocks displayed together can make a touching vignette.

what you'll need

DecoArt Patio Paints in Wrought Iron Black · Cloud White · Sunflower Yellow · Patio Brick · Pinecone Brown · Daisy Cream · Geranium Red · small stiff-bristled flat brush · small round and stipplers or stenciling brushes · white-leaded pencil · template-making supplies, listed on page 10, optional · clear acrylic spray sealer

1 | Select a Rock

When selecting a rock, consider the way lambs' ears extend out from either side of the head. Choose a rock with a surface broad enough to accommodate those ears. All three of these rocks have a slight hump that suggests the top of the head, and enough breadth to fit almost horizontal ears. I chose the center rock for this project.

2 | Paint the Basecoat

Mix two parts white with two black, and add in one part Sunflower Yellow to warm up the mixture. Basecoat the rock with a stiff-bristled brush. When the paint is dry use a white-leaded pencil or soapstone pen to sketch on the features.

3 | Sketch the Design

For lambs, the head and haunch circles are similar in diameter. Draw a smaller circle for the muzzle and place it slightly below the center of the head. Align the eyes and the bottoms of the ears along the top of the muzzle.

Refer to these drawings again when you're painting for guidance on placement of the shading and on fur direction.

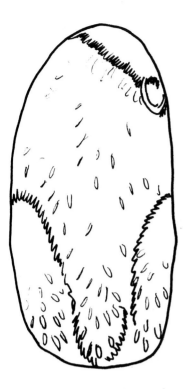

4| Establish Soft Contours

Combine equal parts black paint and Patio Brick to make a deep brown. Apply by pressing or "pouncing" with a short, scruffy brush, one whose bristles are worn and separated. If you don't have such a brush, try using a deerfoot stippler or a small stencil brush. Hold the brush perpendicular to the rock surface and apply the paint with short stabbing motions, turning the brush as you work for a random look. Start on the backside of the rock to get a feel for this technique. Go around the outside edges of your guidelines, giving them bold outlines that are widest in areas that will be shadowed, like the crook of the back leg.

5| Add Contours to Front

Paint contours around all the features on the front side of the rock, adding extra shadows below the ears, along the lower half of the muzzle circle and below the head circle. Darken inside both ears. Shadow more heavily the crook of the leg and the area just above the folded front legs. Contour the forehead lightly with a curved line of shadowing just above and between the eyes. A light scattering of these pressed-on strokes adds texture to the lower half of the haunches and to the lower half of the chest.

6| Add Lighter Color

Building up layers of several colors helps achieve the fluffy look of lamb's wool. Mix together equal parts Pinecone Brown and Daisy Cream. Apply this color most heavily to the tops of elements: the top curve of the head and the haunches, the tops of the rear legs and the tops of the folded front legs. Also use it along the top of the muzzle and the outside edges of the cheek areas as well as on the lamb's back along the top of the rock. Pounce this on as you did with the shadows, pressing the paint on lightly and turning the brush often to get an almost lacy texture.

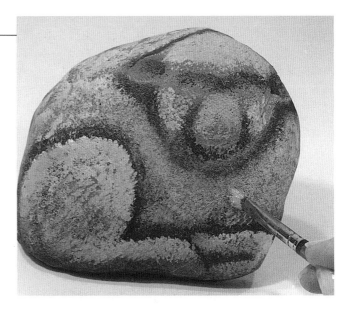

7| Fill in the Ears

To paint the insides of the ears, begin with a drop of Daisy Cream and add in tiny increments of Geranium Red and Sunflower Yellow to get a warm pink. Use a small round brush to cover the insides of both ears. Avoid covering the shadowed base, and leave the dark outlines in place around the edges to define the ears.

8| Paint White Layers on the Back

On the top half of the rock, use your worn brush and pure white paint to give the lamb a diffused layer of white. Begin at the lower reaches with sparse strokes. As you near the top of the rock, gradually apply the white almost solidly.

Switch to a short round brush with soft bristles to add short fat strokes to the haunch. Unlike fur lines, begin these at the outside edges of the haunch by setting the brush tip down solidly then pulling inward to create a teardrop shape. These strokes should be sparse and random in the bottom half, becoming denser as your work up toward the top of the curve. Use the same short, fat strokes to detail the top of the folded-over front leg on that side.

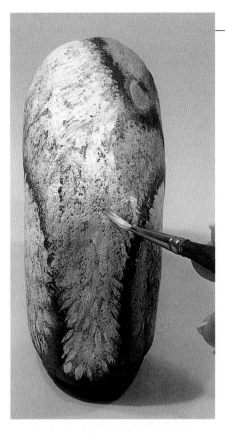

9| Add White to the Tail

Give the tail texture as you did at the haunch, then return to the scruffy brush to fill in the rest of the back. Turn your rock around and detail the fleece on the front haunch and front side in the same way.

10| Paint the Head

Once the body is covered, use the pure white paint on your small round brush to fill in the top of the head with short, thick strokes, leaving just enough space between strokes to give them definition. When the top of the head is covered, outline around the shapes of the eyes with pure white, and go around the outside edges of the ears without covering the dark outlines made earlier.

11| Add More Fleecy Texture

Switch to Daisy Cream to surround the outside of the face with stubby strokes, working inward with subsequent layers until you reach the shadows encircling the muzzle. Use the same color to give more texture to the edges of the front and back legs. Careful layering on of these fat strokes is what gives the lamb its fleecy texture.

12| Fill in the Muzzle Area

Use a small stiff-bristled brush and white paint, wiping away excess pigment so what remains must be scrubbed on. Fill in the muzzle this way, giving the area a soft look while leaving very narrow, dark margins in place for definition. Leave the small V-shaped nose uncovered as well as the lines for the mouth and the vertical connection between mouth and nose. Switch to a liner brush to outline the top of the nose and to fill in the chin with solid white.

13| Fine Tune the Features

Use a liner brush and black paint to go over the mouth line, to underline the nose V and the straight line connecting it to the mouth below. Fill in the eye circles, keeping them small and oval, with short extensions from the outside top edges and down from the inside corners.

14| Detail the Hooves

Still using black paint and your liner brush, outline around the edges of the two back hooves and add a line down the center to create the characteristic split hoof this animal has.

15| Adding More Texture

Now is the time to look over your lamb and determine what areas are in need of more fleecy texture. Scatter fat, very white strokes over the chest, sides and haunch, and any place that seems to need more texture. You can also mix up some medium gray paint and use it sparingly to add fleecy texture in areas where the dark basecoat was covered too completely to provide any contrast. Scattering narrow J-shaped lines about at varying angles makes them appear to be shadowing thick fleecy wool.

16| Finish the Eyes

A tiny dot of white in the center of each eye gives the lamb a life-like gleam.

Allow the paint to dry, then spray the rock with clear acrylic sealer to heighten the colors and protect the paint.

More zoo animals to paint

Make a goat and her kid to join your lamb at the petting zoo!

Mother Goat With Kid

On a rock similar to those used for lambs, you can paint this appealing pair. I used combinations of Patio Brick, Sunflower Yellow and Cloud White to paint and detail the mother. For the kid I chose to use black and shades of gray plus white, while mimicking the mother's markings so that they are similar but different.

Resources

Part of the appeal of rock painting is that the surfaces are easy to find and the materials are simple and few. Most of the materials used are available at any craft or hardware store. However, if you are unable to locate a product, contact the manufacturer below for information on a retailer near you.

Paints
DecoArt Patio Paints
P.O. Box 386
Stanford, KY 40484
www.decoart.com

Brushes
Loew-Cornell
563 Chestnut Ave.
Teaneck, NJ 07666-2490
201-836-7070
www.loew-cornell.com

Wood Filler
Leech's Real Wood Filler
Leech Products
P.O. Box 2147
Hutchinson, KS 67504
620-669-0145 or 800-992-9018
www.leechadhesives.com

Adhesives
Bond Adhesives Company
Newark, NJ 07114
800-879-0527

Index

Paint more whimsical rock art
with Lin Wellford

Anyone can paint unique little works of art with this guide. 11 step-by-step projects are included, plus inspiring ideas for many more!

ISBN 0-89134-572-8
paperback, 128 pages
#30606-K

Transform rocks of all sizes and shapes into dazzling flowers that will bloom year round.

ISBN 0-89134-945-6
paperback, 128 pages
#31373-K

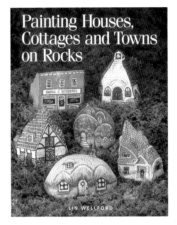

Create a unique array of miniature houses and villages on ordinary rocks. No special skills are required to get fabulous results!

ISBN 0-89134-720-8
paperback, 128 pages
#30823-K

Young artists will have tons of fun painting 10 colorful projects such as tropical fish, teddy bears and lizards. This kid-friendly introduction includes easy patterns and photos to foster creativity and inspiration.

ISBN 1-58180-255-2
paperback, 64 pages
#32085-K

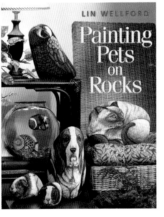

Everyone can create amazing three-dimensional portraits of beloved pets with these 11 projects. Wellford gives you tips on using family photos to achieve lifelike results and includes a gallery of popular and exotic pets.

ISBN 1-58180-032-0
paperback, 128 pages
#31552-K

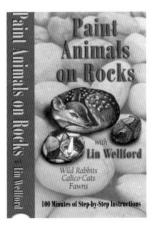

Lin Wellford's wildly popular rock art painting is now on video! Three of her favorite projects are demonstrated from start to finish. She also includes tips on selecting rocks, laying out the pattern, and all of the information needed to bring each piece to life.

ISBN 0-9700713-0-2
100-minute VHS Video
#31836-K